Richard Mathews

A Series of Letters on the Public Service

On the Coast of Coromandel from August 1778, to March 1779

Richard Mathews

A Series of Letters on the Public Service
On the Coast of Coromandel from August 1778, to March 1779

ISBN/EAN: 9783337021146

Printed in Europe, USA, Canada, Australia, Japan

Cover: Foto ©ninafisch / pixelio.de

More available books at **www.hansebooks.com**

A SERIES of LETTERS

ON THE

PUBLIC SERVICE,

ON THE

COAST of *COROMANDEL*,

From *August* 1778, to *March* 1779.

of LETTERS

N THE

SERVICE,

N THE

COROMANDEL,

1778, to *March* 1779.

DON:
MBERT, in the STRAND.
MDCC.LXXX.

A SERIES of LETTERS

ON THE

PUBLIC SERVICE,

ON THE

COAST of *COROMANDEL*,

From *August* 1778, to *March* 1779.

———————

LONDON:
Printed for L. LAMBERT, in the STRAND.
M.DCC.LXXX.

Extract of Orders from Europe, *as settled by a General Court of Proprietors,* October 14, 1778.

THAT all orders within the garrison of Fort William and town of Calcutta, except such as relate to regimental detail, and to military discipline, or to the defence of the fort, be given in the name of the governor-general, who shall keep the keys of the fort and give the parole; but orders respecting regimental detail and discipline of the army in general, including the garrison of fort William, and troops stationed in the town of Calcutta, shall be given in the name of the military commander in chief, or in his absence, in the name of the superior military officer doing duty at fort William, for the time being, who shall communicate all such orders to the governor-general, by his aid de camp, or other proper officer, for his approbation, before they be issued to the troops in the said garrison, or in the town of Calcutta.

Paragraph 42.

That, in case of the attack of any subordinate factory in Bengal, Bahar, or Orissa, the keys be delivered to the commander in chief, or in his absence, to the superior military officer present at such factory; the mode of defence left entirely to his judgment, and the whole executive military power be vested in him, till the enemy shall

shall be expelled, subject, however, at all times, to the controul of the governor-general and council, or of the military commander in chief.

54. That the commander in chief, or superior military officer, in every district, be expressly ordered by the governor-general and council to comply with such requisitions as shall be made by the company's chief civil servants, for troops in all cases where military assistance may be necessary; and in every such requisition, the chief civil servants shall explain to the military officer, in writing, so far as it may be practicable, the nature of the service to be performed; but the mode of carrying it into execution, and the number of troops and quantity of stores requisite for that purpose, shall be determined by the chief and council, in all subordinates where there shall not be an establishment of a chief and council, the same shall be left to the judgment of the military officer in whom the executive power is vested.

Orders from Madras.

1st, The keys of the subordinate settlement Ganjam, Vizagapatam, Masulipatam and Cuddalore, to be kept by the company's chief civil servant, who is also to give out the parole, and to receive returns of the troops in such settlements from the military commanding officers, until the settlement shall be attacked, when the keys shall be delivered to the commander in chief, or in his absence, to the superior military officer present at such settlement; the mode of defence left entirely to his judgment, and the whole executive military power vested in him, till the enemy shall be repelled, subject, however, at all times, to the controul of the governor and council, or of the military commander in chief.

2dly, To make returns to the chief and council; comply with requisitions; and to correspond with them.

Queries

Queries put by Sir Robert Fletcher *to General* Clavering, *with General* Clavering's *Answers.*

Query 1. Can General Clavering remove any man or men from one corps to another, without the approbation of the chiefs and councils in districts under the subordinates? or, can he make such removals in the other corps in the army, without first applying to the board?

Answer. The commander in chief, by virtue of the 42d article of the company's instructions, removes officers and soldiers from one corps to another, as he imagines it will be most conducive to military discipline and the good of the service, without either applying to the chiefs of subordinates, or to the board. This authority was exercised before his arrival, either by the commander in chief or by the governor.

Query 2. Do General Clavering's orders from Calcutta, to the troops at Patna, and the other subordinates, go thro' the chiefs and councils? and do such orders receive any authority but that of general Clavering, before they go from the presidency?

Answer. When resolutions are taken in council, which regard the army, a transcript of those resolutions is sent to the military commander in chief by the secretary, and he issues them to every brigade, and to every station, including the residences of of the chiefs and councils.—General Clavering's orders never go through the chiefs and councils, nor do they receive any authority but that which is above-mentioned.

Query 3. If general Clavering were at or near a subordinate, is he subject to any orders but those of the Governor general and council?

Answer. The commander in chief is not subject to the orders of the chief and council, either at or near the subordinate. He and all commanding officers are directed by the 54th article of the instructions, to comply with such requisitions as shall be made by the company's chief civil servants for troops. In drawing up this article, the court of directors have strictly

strictly conformed to the practice in England, where all military officers are directed to lend assistance, when required, to the civil officers. General Clavering thinks himself not subject to any other orders in Bengal, but those of the Governor-general and council, excepting such as he may receive from the honourable the court of Directors.

Query 4. Who grants leave of absence to officers in and near to Patna, and other places, where there is a chief and council? and can general Clavering grant such leave, independent of the chief and councils?

Answer. The chief and council, at Patna, or at any other place within these provinces, do not grant leave of absence to officers. Conformable to the 45th paragraph of the court of Directors' instructions, temporary leave of absence is granted by the Governor-general to officers doing duty in the garrison of fort William, or town of Calcutta, and by the military commander in chief of the company's forces in Bengal, Bahar, and Orissa, to all other officers. No doubt can arise on the interpretation of this article.

Query 5. *This query and the answer being the same as Case* 1*st, seems improper; but it is conformable to the original.*

Query 6. Can the chiefs and council of subordinates order court martials?

Answer. By a warrant, dated March 30, 1763, the governor and council of each presidency are impowered by the court of Directors, by virtue of a warrant from the king, to authorise the commander in chief of each detachment of their forces, to hold courts martial: I conceive courts martial

[5]

Query 7. *This query is twice repeated in* Sir Robert Fletcher's *Minute.*

Query 8. Is it general Clavering, or the board, that grants leave of abfence to Paymafters and furgeons of corps ftationed out of Calcutta and fort William?

martial held by any other authority, to be illegal.

Anfwer. The paymafters and furgeons are confidered as forming part of the army. *Vide* anfwer to Query (quoted on Cafe 2d) beginning, " Who grants leave of abfence, &c."

A true Copy, taken from the authentic Records, publifhed by order of the Company.

Wm. SYDENHAM.

Fort St. George, Dec. 22, 1778.

Whereas many and great inconveniences have arifen to the public fervice by difputes between the Company's chief, civil and military fervants, at the fubordinate fettlements, refpecting the feparate military powers vefted in each ; and whereas in the feveral contefts that have unhappily been raifed on this fubject, it appears evident, that the military fervants have, in general, not only exceeded the bounds of their juft authority, but have thrown off the appearance of that refpect, and deference, which the company's orders, and the neceffity of the fervice require to be paid to the chief civil fervants, intrufted with the directions and management of their affairs, at the fubordinate fettlements ; the honourable the Prefident and Select Committee, viewing thofe proceedings in a moft ferious and important light, and being extremely defirous of putting a ftop to the confufion that has already refulted from them, of reftoring the authority of the company's chief civil fervants, and tracing fuch a clear, and ftrong line, as may be moft likely to prevent all future mifunderftandings, have thought proper to come to the following refolutions, which are to be implicitly obeyed.

General Orders iffued by the Select Committee.

1ft,

1st, The keys of the subordinate settlements, Ganjam, Masulipatam, Vizagapatam, and in general all other places, where the company have chiefs and councils, or residents, are to be kept by the chief civil servant in those places respectively, who is to give out the parole, and to receive returns of troops in such settlements, from the military commanding officer: but in case such settlement be attacked, then the keys shall be delivered to the superior military officer present, at such settlement, and the mode of defence left entirely to his judgment, and the whole executive power vested in him, until the enemy shall be repulsed, (subject, however, at all times, to the controul of the president and select committee, or of the military commander in chief) but when the enemy shall be repelled, such power shall cease, and the keys of the garrison delivered back to the chief civil servant.

2dly, The chiefs, and councils, or residents in those settlements where troops are, or may be stationed, are from henceforth to have the entire direction and controul of those troops, (subject only to the authority of the select committee, and to the exceptions hereafter mentioned, with respect to the powers of the commander in chief) they are to order and employ them upon any service they may find expedient, and to give them such instructions as they may think proper, relative to the mode of executing such service, which are to be implicitly obeyed.

3dly, The commander in chief of the army being vested with authority to publish, in his own name, all orders respecting the regimental detail and discipline of the troops in general. The company's chief civil servants, at the subordinate settlements, are in no respect to interfere in matters of this nature, such order, however, as may be thus issued in the name of the commander in chief, are not to be issued in any of the subordinate settlements, until they shall have

have been first countersigned by the chief civil servant; nor shall any garrison order whatever, be published by or in the name of the commandant of the troops in such subordinacies, without being first approved and signed by the chief civil servant.

4th, All resolutions passed by the select committee, concerning the promotion, or dismission, of military officers, and, in general, all such as they may think proper to signify in general orders to the army, are to be communicated as usual to the commander in chief, and by him circulated to all the troops, except those within the garrison of Fort St. George; but with respect to the troops doing duty in the subordinate settlements, and their dependencies, copies of such general orders will be sent by the secretary to the chiefs, and councils, or residents, in such settlements, for their information.

5thly, All military commanding officers of troops, within, and dependent upon, the subordinate settlements, are to make regular returns to the chiefs, and councils, or residents, and to correspond with them upon all matters respecting the service, except such as relate to regimental detail, or military discipline.

6thly, The commander in chief, being vested with authority to grant temporary leave of absence, in time of peace, to all officers doing duty out of the garrison, of Fort St. George, such leave of absence, with respect to the officers within, and dependent upon the several subordinate settlements, is in future to be sent by the commander in chief, under a flying seal, to the chiefs, and councils, or residents, that they may know to whom such leave is given; and every officer, within their respective dependencies, who shall avail himself of such leave of absence, is to give notice to them, both at his departure and his return; and if leave of absence be given to any officer doing duty in the principal garrisons of a subordinate settlement,

tlement, he is not to avail himself of it, without waiting upon the chief and reporting his departure to him; he must also, at his return, immediately report himself to the chief.

7thly, The president and select committee have resolved, that in future there shall be no commanding officer whose authority shall extend to the troops within, and dependent upon, any subordinate settlement, unless by special appointment; but that each officer shall command the batallion, or corps, to which he may be attached, and confine himself to that only, unless when the troops of different batallions, or corps, are doing duty together; and then the senior officer is of course to command.

8thly, No military officer in the Circars, is, on any account to correspond with the country powers, or with any of the Rajahs, or Zemindars, except on service in the field; and in such cases where it might be prejudicial to wait for applications through the regular channel of the chief and council; but in these cases, the correspondence must be confined to the particular service in which such officer may be employed, and a copy of it must be transmitted by the first opportunity to the chief and council, under whose orders he may be acting at the time.

By order of the President and Select Committee,

Signed,   *Charles Oakley*, Secretary.

                     J. Burrowes, Adjutant-general.

Extract of the Company's General Letter to Fort St. George, dated paragr. 41.
January 30, 1778. Sent per Osterly, Grosvenor, &c.

Although, in our advices of last year, we found ourselves under the necessity of promoting Mr. Alex. Maclellan to a Majority in your infantry establishment, in consequence of his having been aid de camp to General Wedderburn, who unfortunately fell in our service on the Malabar coast; we, nevertheless, feel an anxiety in having so done, in prejudice to an officer of so much real merit as captain Richard Mathews, whom we find has served us for upwards of eighteen years upon your establishment. In order, therefore, to relieve, in some degree, his feelings upon such a supercession, it is our positive direction, that you take the earliest opportunity of giving him a mark of our favour.

Copy of a Letter from Generals sir Eyre Coote, John Caillaud, and Joseph Smith, to the Court of Directors.

Gentlemen,

Respect to ourselves, as well as the board we are addressing, would render the appearance of any interference in your resolutions very irksome to us, were not the present application dictated by the principles with which we have always served the company, and have seen the good effect.

The fortune of an officer, who has long and continually served with spirit, zeal, and activity, must be precious to those who, by the honour of commanding your troops, are convinced of his merit, by personal and immediate knowledge, we intercede for captain Mathews, who is in England, solliciting to recover the loss of rank which he has sustained by the appointment of captain Maclellan from that rank at Bombay, to a Majority on the coast of Coromandel.

The private merits of Mr. Maclellan are not our object. It is a rule to suppose that every officer under equal circumstances might have rendered *equal* services.

Captain Mathews has served under the one or the other of us, in a course of eighteen years, in the cavalry and infantry, and with such approbation, that, were the same occasions to revert, we should give the preference over him to no officer of equal rank on your establishment.

It may be the boast of the India Company, that the rotation of merit has in no military service in the world been preserved with more equity than in theirs; We, therefore, flatter ourselves that this our representation in favour of an *officer* so deserving of the company's attention, will meet with due consideration from the honourable the court of Directors, whom, we are sensible, wish to give every encouragement to *officers*, meriting their countenance and protection.

We have the honour to be, with great respect,

 Gentlemen,

  Your most obedient, and much obliged humble servants,

   Signed   *Eyre Coote,*

           John Caillaud,

London, March 10, 1778.   *Joseph Smith.*

The Select Committee, to Major Mathews.

Sir,

Having appointed you to command the troops in the Mafulipatam diftrict, you are to proceed thither with all poffible expedition; and we inclofe you a letter for the chief and council, to be delivered on your arrival.

In addition to the troops now in the Mafulipatam diftrict, we have ordered a battalion from Chicacole, and two companies from Ongole. We have alfo directed, that the invalids, which came with captain Collins from Mafulipatam, with one lieutenant fireworker, one ferjeant, and twelve artillery men, fhall be left at Ongole, and remain there until they receive your orders to march back to the Mafulipatam diftrict, when they are to be accompanied by the fepoys ordered from Ongole.

We have recommended to the chief and council at Mafulipatam, to give you all the affiftance in their power, and directed captain Barclay at Ongole, and captain Philips, who commands for the Nabob at Palnaud, to correfpond with you upon all matters relative to the fervice.

We defire you particularly to watch the motions of Mr. Lally, who has a confiderable force in the Guntoor Circar, and to act with the troops under your command in the beft manner poffible for the defence of the company's diftricts, or occafionally on the offenfive againft the French troops with Mr. Lally, as the circumftances of affairs may render moft eligible, advifing us, and the chief and council of Mafulipatam regularly of your proceedings, and of all material intelligence you may be able to procure.

Having resolved to raise two more batallions of sepoys for the Circars, we desire you will endeavour all in your power to procure recruits for them.

We are, sir,
  Your most obedient servants,

Fort St. George,
  Aug. 7, 1778.

Thomas Rumbold,
John Whitehill,
Charles Smith.

The Select Committee, to Major Mathews, commanding in the Masulipatam district.

Sir,

Should captain Collins's detachment be north of the Kistna, on your arrival at Masulipatam, we desire you will take the direction of it, until you shall esteem it to be out of danger of any attempt, that might be made by Mr. Lally's party from the Guntoor Circar.

We are, sir,
  Your most obedient servants,

Fort St. George,
  Aug. 9, 1778.

Thomas Rumbold,
John Whitehill,
Charles Smith.

The Select Committee, to Major Mathews, commanding the troops in the Circars.

Sir,

I am directed by the president and select committee to send you the accompanying warrant, empowering you to assemble general courts martial, for the trial of offences committed in that part of the troops under your command.

By a general order of the 4th ult. no sentence of a general court martial is to be carried into execution without the approbation of the board; but I am directed to acquaint you, that the president and select committee, in consideration of the distance between your

station

station and the presidency, and confiding in your judgment and discretion, have granted you full power to carry into execution the sentence of any court martial that may be held by your appointment.

I am, sir, your most obedient servant,

D. Baine, dep. sec.

Fort St. George, Aug. 16, 1778.

The Select Committee, to Major Mathews, commanding the troops in the Masulipatam Circar.

Sir,

Our squadron under the command of sir Edward Vernon having driven the French fleet out of the road of Pondicherry, they have sailed northward, with intention, we apprehend, to make a diversion on some part of the coast. We direct, therefore, that you take proper measures to secure the company's possessions in the Circars from insult; attending particularly to the security of the fort of Masulipatam and port of Coringy.

We recommend it to you to take your measures in such manner as may give as little alarm to the country as possible.

We are, sir, your most obedient servants,

Thomas Rumbold,
John Whitehill,
Charles Smith.

Fort St. George, Aug. 22, 1778.

The Select Committee, to Major Mathews, commanding the troops in the Masulipatam Circars.

Sir,

Since writing to you last night, we have received further intelligence of the French fleet, which, for the present, removes the apprehension we expressed to you. It is, therefore, unnecessary, until

til you hear further from us, to make any alteration in the arrangement before laid down for the troops under your command.

We are, fir, your moſt obedient ſervants,

Thomas Rumbold,
John Whitehill,
Charles Smith.

Fort St. George, Aug. 23, 1778.

General Munro, to Major Mathews.

Sir,

I am favoured with your letter of the 4th of September. As the order of the 12th of Auguſt was approved and iſſued by the ſelect committee, I cannot defer the promotion of the Jemadars, Havaldars, Naikes, and ſepoys, removed from other battalions; but when the returns for promotion come to me, I ſhall forward them: I do not expect that the battalions that give men for promotion, will give the beſt they have; but at the ſame time I cannot think they will recommend thoſe that are unworthy.

Your obſervations, relative to the improper uſe made of the ſepoys, is very juſt; and unleſs proper means are uſed to prevent this abuſe, the Circar battalions will be effectually ruined, inſpite of every attention that the officers can pay to their duty.

If this rupture had not happened, I intended viſiting the Circars; not only to judge of the country, but to endeavour to aboliſh the very abuſes you mention; and I hope ſtill to have it in my power to purſue my intentions.

No alteration can poſſibly take place as to eſtabliſhment of battalions, nor would I wiſh to ſee fewer officers than the ſepoy battalions have. The European invalids were formed into a battalion juſt before this expedition took place, and, therefore, they were not all collected. It was intended to have purſued ſome plan of the like

nature

nature for the sepoys; and which will still be carried into execution, as soon as time will permit." In the mean time, you may order such men as are unfit for field duty, to garrison duty, finding proper officers to take charge of them. Your reasons for the weakness of the battalions is very proper, with respect to the absentees on revenue duty, recruits and other men; as also the divided state of the battalions: bad black officers may arise from several reasons. By a late arrangement there will be one European officer to each company. It is time must make them understand their business; for the European battalions that should be well supported, are almost ruined by officers that have served, being removed to sepoy batallions.

I have the honour to be, sir,
Your most obedient servant,
Hector Munro.

Camp near Pondicherry, Sept. 22, 1778.

General Munro, to Major Mathews.

Sir,

I am favoured with your letter of the 29th of August. I am very sensible how detrimental it is to the public service, that sepoys should be employed in collecting the revenue, when Peons, as you observe, would answer much better.

I thank you for your information concerning Mr. Lally; I hope he will remain quiet; but be assured, that if we are successful against Pondicherry, the instant that the siege is over, the Circar grenadiers shall be ordered to the northward.

I entirely approve of the disposition you have made of the troops. Should you hear any thing more of Mr. Lally's motions, you will please to inform me.

I have the honour to be, sir,
Your most obedient servant,
Hector Munro.

Camp before Pondicherry, Sept. 6, 1778.

To

The Select Committee, to Major Mathews, commanding the troops in the diſtrict of Maſulipatam.

Sir,

We have received your ſeveral letters, and are much concerned at the diſputes which have ariſen between the chief and council of Maſulipatam and you, as we fear they may materially injure the public ſervice, at a time when all our endeavours are required to promote and forward it to the utmoſt.

In expectation that theſe diſputes will immediately ceaſe, and perfect harmony be reſtored, we ſhall proceed to communicate to you our opinions upon the points in difference, and to notice ſuch parts of your conduct as appear exceptionable.

We intended that the chief and council ſhould follow your recommendation and opinion, in reſpect to the arrangement of troops for the ſecurity of the diſtrict; but we meant alſo that you ſhould pay a proper regard to their ſentiments and advice, which you appear not to have done; and we are ſorry to remark, a want of reſpect on your part, in declining to attend their board when deſired to do ſo. The reaſons aſſigned by you, on this occaſion, are not ſatisfactory, and we think, had you attended, you would have manifeſted a ſtronger inclination to come to an agreement with the chief and council, than you appear to have done by your refuſal.

In regard to the requiſition for troops, which was ſent from the chief and council a few days after your arrival, without being communicated to you, we have expreſſed to them our opinion, that they acted improperly; but, at the ſame time, we cannot paſs unnoticed the diſreſpectful ſtyle of your letter to them, in conſequence, wherein you ſpeak of that proceeding in terms very reprehenſible.

As to the reſt, your withdrawing the ſepoys employed on the revenue ſervice, without the concurrence of the chief and council; your

your ordering the delivery and removal of stores from Ellore, without authority from them, directing captain Rowles to address them in the manner he has done, with respect to the Lascars of the garrison, without considering or writing to them on the subject, and omitting to furnish them with advice concerning your operations until they had been in part executed, whereby they were deprived of the opportunity of giving you their sentiments in time upon such points as might require them, are all disrespectful and unauthorised proceedings, which we cannot suffer to pass unnoticed.

The chief and council are the persons charged under us with the interests and affairs of the company, in the Circars. They are left to be the judges when military assistance is necessary for the purposes of the revenue or any other service; and are empowered to make requisitions, which on the part of the commanding officer are to receive implicit obedience.

It was not within your province to determine whether the troops which had been required and employed on the revenue service were necessary, or might be recalled; much less was it so to proceed to the actual recall of them without any authority whatever, and without knowing what detriment it might cause to the collections.

The arrangement and issues of stores also compose a part of the duty of the chief and council, and not a single article is permitted to be delivered for use, or removed from place to place, without their express orders. We are surprised that this circumstance should have been unknown to you, or that you should have disregarded it in the manner you appear to have done. In future no stores are to be delivered to you without a regular indent to the chief and council, or removed from place to place, without their authority.

In respect to the letter addressed by captain Rowles to the chief and council of Masulipatam, in consequence of your orders, the

manner

manner of this proceeding is on your own part disrespectful. The Lascars are entirely under the direction of the chief and council. Your ordering captain Rowles to consider them as part of the strength of the garrison, and to require an account of their number, how employed, &c. without previously consulting with the chief and council yourself, or desiring their permission to include them in the strength of the garrison, was evidently passing beyond the bounds of your authority, at the same time that it was disrespectful, and tended to widen the breach between you.

A due consideration of all these circumstances has determined us to alter our former intentions so far as to direct that, whilst you remain in the Masulipatam district, your correspondence shall not be addressed to us and the chief and council, but to the latter only, before whom you are to lay all your plans of operations, intelligence, &c. Such orders as we may have occasion to send you will pass through the chief and council; but all requisitions they may think proper to make for military assistance are to be implicitly obeyed; and you are instantly to return whatever number of sepoys they may require for the service of the collections. We have desired them in future to send their requisitions immediately to you, unless in particular cases, where the service might be injured by delay, and for these you are to make provision by giving the necessary orders to the several officers in command.

As we do not find by the latest intelligence we have received, that Mr. Lally is moving from Adoni, we are of opinion, that it is unnecessary to make any detachments from your force at present, as it may give much alarm to the inhabitants, and injure the collection of the revenues. We desire, therefore, that you will fix your camp in some proper situation for the security of the district, and not move any troops towards the Guntoor Circar, without further orders, or without the concurrence of the chief and council of Masulipatam.

In

In the present situation of Mr. Lally, we think too that the signals you have established, to give notice of the approach of an enemy, may necessarily alarm the inhabitants, and should, therefore, be discontinued for the present.

We are, sir, your most obedient servants,

Thomas Rumbold,
John Whitehill,
Charles Smith.

Fort St. George, Sept. 6, 1778.

Captain Powell, to Major Mathews.

The following is, to the best of my recollection, the purport of conversation between Major Mathews, and Yencanah Dourah, the 2d of September, at Gundoor, where the Major released him.

Major Mathews informed Yencanah Dourah, through Langum Dourah, his Dubash, that if he promised to return immediately home, and there remain quiet, and not interfere in any shape with the management of the country, and oblige his son Rajanah Dourah to discharge his Peons, and other fighting people, and do the same, he would release him; the Major further told him, by such behaviour his son might, perhaps, get possession of his country again; but that if either he, his son, or any of the family, should offer to commit any depredations in any part of the country belonging to the honourable company, should he, or they, be taken, they must expect no mercy.

Yencanah Dourah then gave Major Mathews, in writing, a promise of his good behaviour; at which time the Major delivered to him a small box of gold and silver jewels, and two crosses, which were found with him when he was taken by lieutenant M'Gill. Major Mathews directed me to give from my battalion, a Naigue and four sepoys, as an escort, to see him as far as he chose on his way homeward.

James Powell.

Ellore, October 8, 1778.

Mr. Rumbold, to Major Mathews.

Sir,

I have received your favour of the 4th, and cannot on any account approve of your having released Yencanah Dourah, without the knowledge and consent of the chief and council of Masulipatam. He was confined by them, and with the approbation of this government, and your advice to him to wait the justice of the new chief Mr. Cotesford, was certainly a reflection on the gentlemen at present in the direction of affairs at Masulipatam, equally unnecessary and improper, without you had very sufficient proofs of any injustice from them towards him; and even then it would have been right, in the first instance, to have made such a representation, as might have given the gentlemen an opportunity of vindicating themselves.

I am, sir, your most obedient servant,

Thomas Rumbold.

Fort St. George, Sept. 20, 1778.

General Munro, to Major Mathews.

Sir,

I am favoured with your letter of the 12th of September, and I think the disposition you made of the troops under your command was most judicious. The reason for their being ordered to re-cross the Kistna, I am not as yet acquainted with. I should be very sorry any misunderstanding should arise between the select committee and you; nor can I imagine any such thing can happen, as I hope they are satisfied as well as I am of your having acted with the

greatest

greatest attention for the service of the company. In the 54th paragraph of the company's instructions it mentions, that the commanding officer in every district is ordered to comply with such requisitions as shall be made by the company's chief civil servant for troops in all cases, where military assistance may be necessary, &c.

My construction of that order is, that the officers commanding troops are implicitly to comply with requisitions made by the chief civil servant; but at the same time, no such requisitions can be made, unless the service of the company require military assistance: and therefore no orders respecting the motion or discipline of the troops given by the officer commanding are to be impeded by any chief or council in a subordinate settlement; but that the troops are subject to all orders from the governor and select committee at Madras; or such as by authority they may receive from the commander in chief.

To obviate, therefore, every difficulty in your situation, I recommend it to you to state your reasons for your conduct, as an officer commanding the troops in a particular district, and send it to Madras, desiring that it may remain on record, in case your conduct in this business might hereafter be subject to enquiry. I have sent a copy of this letter to the select committee.

I have the honour to be, sir,

Your most obedient humble servant,

Hector Munro.

Camp before Pondicherry, Sept. 24, 1778.

General Munro, to Major Mathews.

Sir,

As captain Bridges was appointed last January only to the command of Condapilly, and was called from it by you, I should be glad

he

he got his command again as soon as you can with propriety send him to it. He is strongly recommended to me as a very deserving good officer; I shall, therefore, be glad to serve him, if possible.

The board have thought proper to make new regulations and alterations in the military department. I have entered two minutes upon it, copies of which Major Campbell will send you.

I am respectfully, sir,

Your most obedient humble servant,

Hector Munro.

Fort St. George, Dec. 23, 1778.

Letters from Major Mathews, to General Munro.

Sir,

The gentleman whom I took the liberty of mentioning to you, as one very sufficient to command the garrison sepoys at Vizagapatam, was first lieutenant of artillery at St. Helena his name is James Molloy. He, by permission of the court of Directors, accompanied me from England.

I have been examining the returns of the troops under Ganjam and Vizagapatam, and find that, in respect to the number stationed in each district, I was mistaken. Four companies are the most that can with propriety be drawn from Asha; these may be fixed at Vizagapatam or Cicacole. One battalion may then be taken from the Cicacole Circar to reinforce the troops under Masulipatam. The battalions in the Cicacole Circar are (in effectives) very weak, as appears by the last returns. If it be thought necessary to make these removes, there will then remain under the several chiefships as follows:

At Ganjam, &c. one company of Coffres, and twelve companies of sepoys, exclusive of garrison sepoys.

At

At Vizagapatam, &c. twelve companies of sepoys, and two companies of garrison sepoys.

At Masulipatam, &c. forty companies of sepoys.

There must remain in garrison at Masulipatam, at least, eight companies, and at Condapilly, two companies: so that, when the Cicacole battalion joins, thirty companies are the most that can be drawn together; and these, allowing for sickness and other casualties, may not amount to above 1,800 effective men. To strengthen these, you will, sir, forgive me if I presume to hint that four or five companies may be taken from Ongole, as that fort is at a distance from danger, and if threatened by the French party belonging to Basalatjung may be relieved from the northward, whose particular business, I suppose, will be to watch Mr. Lally's motions.

Colonel Cosby tells me, that the artillery men are ordered from Ellore, and that there are not any in the district. I trust, sir, that you will think a few for a small field train highly necessary.

At this period your time will be less taken up in reading my sentiments than to receive them verbally; and they now appear as you wished, only by way of memorandum.

I have the honour to be, with great respect, sir,

Your most obedient humble servant,

Richard Mathews.

Madras, *Aug.* 1, 1778.

Major Mathews, to the Hon. Thomas Rumbold, Esq; Governor of Madras.

Honourable Sir,

Give me leave to request that you will be pleased to order captain Lane's battalion to proceed without loss of time to join me. If
they

they wait until the four companies from Ganjam reach Cicacole, I may not be reinforced from that quarter thefe fix weeks; in which time many fatal circumftances may occur. The companies from Ganjam may be at Cicacole, in twelve days after the departure of captain Lane's battalion, full time enough to guard againft any infurrection. I mention this, becaufe I have heard of the report of *Mr. Lally's party. Should captain Collins's party be north of the Kiftna, upon my arrival, it may be neceffary that I have orders to take them under my direction, to fee them out of danger; particularly, if Lally fhould move to the eaftward.

I beg that you will believe that I have nothing elfe in view than to follow your inftructions. Not a man fhall be detained but whom you permit.

I have defired lieutenant Schouler to go by land, and to wait at Ongole to proceed with the companies ordered from thence.

I am, with great refpect, honourable fir,

Your moft obedient humble fervant,

Richard Mathews.

Madras, Aug. 8, 1778.

Major Mathews, to the Hon. Thomas Rumbold, Efq; Prefident, &c. and Select Committee, at Fort St. George.

Honourable Sir, and Sirs,

I have the honour of informing you that captain Collins's detachment are out of all danger from Lally's party. By the laft information that I received from captain Barclay (which as yet is the only channel of intelligence) Mr. Lally was at Adoni, and preparing to

march

---

* Reported to be in the Guntoor Circar, and that a detachment under Arno was near the fea coaft.

march down to Guntoor; which garrison he has reinforced with six companies of sepoys.

In this part every preparation is making to execute your orders; and I trust, that although the force is small, that nothing material will happen to draw off your attention from a principal object.

Siege of Pondicherry.

The most that I can bring together is about twelve hundred sepoys; and captain Lane's battalion will not add more than three hundred effectives. When the troops are collected I shall be better enabled to inform you of their condition, and, by that time, may have some true intelligence concerning the enemy.

You were pleased to direct that only a battallion should remain in the garrison of Masulipatam; but as the battalions are weaker than you supposed, I have recommended to the chief and council to reinforce it with a company of new sepoys belonging to another battalion.

It was also thought necessary that a party under an officer should be left for the protection of the honourable company's investment at Injeram, which will be done; and alarm posts established in different parts near this place to give information of an enemy's approach, and to have timely succour from the troops in the field.

I have the honour to be, &c.

Richard Mathews.

Masulipatam, Aug. 15, 1778.

Major Mathews, to the honourable Thomas Rumbold, Esq; President, &c. and Select Committee, at Fort St. George.

Honourable Sir, and Sirs,

When I did myself the honour of addressing you the 15th instant, I expected to have been permitted to carry your orders into execution; for although there were appearances of impediments, yet I hoped, upon mature confideration, your orders would have been conftrued in the light you intended.

Upon my arrival I delivered the letter for the chief and council to Mr. Sadleir, which did not appear fo clear as they wifhed; and, in order to explain your directions, as far as lay in my power, I told Mr. Sadleir the purport of affembling the troops, what you wifhed fhould be done, and fhewed him and to Mr. Barnard the written orders that I received from you. Thefe were not fatisfactory, and they feemed unwilling to draw the troops together.

That no time might be loft in putting your orders into execution, I requefted of them firft verbally, and then by letter, dated the 13th inftant, that they would acquaint the feveral commanding officers of your having appointed me to command the troops in the diftrict, and that the officers fhould conformably thereto obey my orders. This they evaded, as you will perceive by the tenor of their anfwer of the fame date. In their addrefs, they required from me a plan of the arrangement of the troops, &c. which I gave in upon the 15th; this was anfwered by their letter of the 16th. All this time nothing was done towards eftablifhing that force you defired might be brought together. On the contrary, after my arrival, they ordered captain Rowles's battalion into the garrifon without advifing me thereof.

Mr. Lally's force is nearly the ftrength that lieutenat Meek informed you. And Bafalet Jung has 4000 horfe not far from Adoni. Should thefe determine to invade the Circar, or to make a diverfion to the fouthward, they might effect either before any troops could be formed to oppofe them; for it may be fourteen days, or more, before captain Powel is at Ellore.

My views in the arrangement of the troops, was, to leave in Mafulipatam captain Rowles's battalion, which is above 400 ftrong in effective men, and a complete company, formed from captain Johnftone's recruits, two-thirds of them being expert in the ufe of their

arms

arms and fit to join the battalion; so that, instead of little more than three hundred, as the chief and council mentions, there would be near five hundred, exclusive of two hundred good Lascars, and some European invalids. Besides these, the sick of captain Rowles's battallion would be daily recovering, and the absentees joining. But it seems,* " that the battalions commanded by the captains Johnstone " and Rowles, and three companies of captain Bridges's, are only " sufficient to protect the fort of Masulipatam against any *present* " *apparent danger*."

If such a force is to be detained, Mr. Lally will not meet with any obstruction to his movements. He may embark his troops for Pondicherry; or, plunder and destroy the Circars, or, attack Timerycotah, or Ongole, with impunity; or, what would be worse, might get within a hundred miles of Madras and raise a powerful diversion in the Carnatic. But, probably, the gentlemen here will not apprehend danger from the west until it is felt; the storm is to gather from the east.

I wanted the garrison of Condapilly reinforced, to enable captain Bridges to march out with five companies and two three pounders, in case that the enemy made any movement towards the banks of the Kistna. This force might take post to prevent the enemy passing the river. Condapilly is about fifty miles from hence; a battalion

(for

---

* The chief and council had demanded such a garrison before my arrival, which amounted to near the whole force then in the district; thirteen weak companies only remaining to garrison the different forts of Samulcotah, Ellore, and Condapilly, to protect a great length of sea-coast, from Jagganautporam, near Samulcotah to China, Ganjam near Ongole, to guard a very extensive frontier, to awe the armed malecontents in the province and the truly respectable party in the Guntoor Circar, and for the purpose of the revenue. From Jagganautporam to Chena Ganjam is more than 200 miles, the communication intercepted by many navigable rivers. Our frontiers in land, towards Hydrabad, is about 150 miles from Masulipatam.

(for the present) stationed half-way, would be ready to act in conjunction with captain Bridges; to succour Masulipatam, should it be threatened from the sea (which is improbable at this time); or, be ready to cross the Kistna, to hang on Lally's rear, should he go to the southward. The part of the Circar, south of the Kistna, would require protection, which the afore-mentioned detachment could afford against an equal force. Should Lally march south, and it appears necessary to follow him immediately, Masulipatam would not be defenceless. There would be seven hundred men in garrison, a number sufficient to secure it from surprise; captain Powell's battalion would be on its march towards it, and captain Lane's following; so that danger would be far distant.

In the arrangement given to the chief and council, I made no mention of a place to form a camp, or general rendezvous. They frequently asked me to name a place, and I always told them that it was out of my power; because it must be determined by the enemy's motions; and it is not certain at this time what route they will take. Their only view in mentioning it, is, to have an opportunity of saying, that Masulipatam might be endangered by the absence of part of its present garrison.*

My answer to their letter is enclosed. I could wish to be enabled to employ my time otherwise than in writing long letters; for it may be detrimental to the service by taking off my attention, and depriving me of the power of defending the Circars, for which purpose I was honoured with the command of the troops.

I must request that your Honours would be pleased to put the matter out of dispute, and (forgive my presumption) word your orders, that they may be understood by the chief and council. For my part I always would wish to act up to the spirit of them, and not seek evasions by grasping at immaterial omissions.

It

---

* Two battalions and a half.

It is impossible for me to say when, even the most trifling encampment will be formed, for my orders may be contradicted, or rendered of no effect by those of the chief and council. All orders for the troops in the Circar, particularly in the time of war, should be issued by me. It is my duty to obey my superiors, which duty I have never been accused of neglecting.

If the defence of the Circars is left to me, or that I am to act offensively against the enemy, my judgment must direct the movements of the troops, the strength and station of posts, otherwise I may be forced into a situation destructive and dishonourable.

That you may form some idea in what manner the troops are dispersed, I inclose two lists of detached parties.

I have the honour, &c.

Richard Mathews.

Masulipatam, Aug. 17, 1778.

Major Mathews, to the Hon. Thomas Rumbold, Esq; President, &c. and Select Committee at Fort St. George.

Honourable Sir, and Sirs,

I am much concerned that I have no better information to give you than the inclosed, which I am induced to send, because the chief and council may not have time to transmit them.

I have hopes that in a few days every thing will be in such order as you will be pleased with an account of.

I have the honour, &c.

Richard Mathews.

Masulipatam, Aug. 19, 1778.

Major

Major Mathews, to the Hon. Thomas Rumbold, Efq; Prefident, &c. and Select Committee, at Fort St. George.

Honourable Sir, and Sirs,

This day the chief and council fent me an extract of a letter they defigned for you, in which I am concerned to find thefe words, " idle expreffions, and vague expreffions, unfupported by facts." Thefe are accufations I never was ufed to, and hope you will think them unmerited. I will not trouble you any more upon fo difagreeable a fubject, when the inclofed intellegence may require your attention.*

I fet off to-morrow morning for Condapilly. Another lift of detached fepoys will further convince you how much they are fcattered in this diftrict. Peons will do as well if the purpofe is only to collect the revenue.

Enclofed is a return of the ftrength of this garrifon, exclufive of thofe that are to march out.

I am forry to inform you, that it is impoffible to raife a battalion in the whole Circars.

I have the honour, &c.

Richard Mathews.

Mafulipatam, Aug. 20, 1778.

Major Mathews, to the Hon. Thomas Rumbold, Efq; Prefident, &c. and Select Committee, at Fort St. George.

Detained againft orders by the connivince of the chief and council.

Honourable Sir, and Sirs,

By a return that I received laft night of the troops, I find there are at Ellore effective artillery of the 5th company, one lieutenant, one

---

* Report of Lally's approach, and that Bafalat Jung was raifing more infantry. See letter to the chief and council, of Auguft 18.

one corporal, two bombardiers, four gunners, and eleven matroſſes, total nineteen. As I underſtood that you had been pleaſed to order every one of that corps from the Circars to Madras, I did not expect to find ſuch a valuable reinforcement at Ellore. I ſhould be glad to know if it is your pleaſure that they ſhould remain in this diſtrict, or ſent to the preſidency, and no more kept here than the number you mentioned to me in my orders. There are alſo two at Maſulipatam that did duty with captain Rowles's battalion.

   I have the honour, &c.

              Richard Mathews.

Maſulipatam Circar, Aug. 21, 1778.

Major Mathews, to the Hon. Thomas Rumbold, Eſq; Preſident, &c. and Select Committee, at Fort St. George.

Honourable Sir, and Sirs,

I have been honoured with your orders of the 22d inſtant. You may be aſſured that every thing ſhall be done that lays in my power for the general ſecurity of the Circars.

A detachment of near two hundred men will be to-morrow or next day at Coringy. Another of ſeven companies, under the command of captain Bridges, will be in the ſame time ſouth of the Kiſtna, to protect our country, and to act as occaſion offers, ſhould any number of troops threaten us from that quarter.

I am endeavouring to collect our ſcattered ſepoys that have been employed money-hunting over the diſtrict. Three-fourths of them cannot be heard of, and I find that I am threatened for doing what I think (particularly at this time, that I cannot collect one thouſand men out of three battalions) an eſſential part of my duty to the honourable company; for any thing that tends to the immediate preſervation of their territory is ſo: ſuch is drawing together between three

                    and

and four hundred men that are living in idleness upon the labour of the poor inhabitants.

The threats are from the chief and council, which I hope you will, as you consider the motive of my acting, be pleased to defend me from, viz.

" The measure you have lately adopted of withdrawing sepoy detachments on revenue service from their stations, will be attended with consequences highly prejudicial to the country and revenue. You will do well, therefore, carefully to weigh this matter; for you must be accountable for all their effects."

I have ordered captain Bridges to write to your Honours whatever may be worthy of information.

I am, with the greatest respect, &c.

Richard Mathews.*

*Camp at Gundoor, 4 miles from
Mafulipatam, Aug. 27, 1778.*

Major Mathews, to General Munro.

Sir,

Agreeably to the orders that I brought from Madras, the troops of this Circar are assembling. But I am sorry to inform you, that it
is

---

* A Return of Sepoys detached over the district of Mafulipatam, said to be employed on Revenue Service, August 1778.

	Jemedars	Havaldars	Naikes	Sepoys	Total
From 2d battalion, from the detachment at Samulcotah	1	7	7	100	115
From 2d battalion, from the detachment at Ellore		3	1	34	38
From 3d battalion, from Mafulipatam	1	3	4	74	82
From 7th battalion, from 4 companies at Condapilly		4	4	95	103
From 7th battalion, from 1 company at Ventapollam				20	20
From 7th battalion, from three companies at Mafulipatam			3	11	14
Straggling Parties Total	2	17	19	334	373

is out of my power to collect the sepoys that are scattered all over the district, under the pretence of the revenue service. Between three and four hundred were absent from their battalions, it is said, for the above purpose; some have not been seen for two years; and about one hundred and fifty cannot at this time be heard of. This business is attended with many bad consequences to the public service, and should be abolished. Peons will answer the purpose much better.

The French party under Mr. Lally, by accounts that are confirmed through different channels, consist of, *viz.*

    150 European horse,
    200 Black cavalry,
    350 European infantry,
    800 Topasses,
   3000 Sepoys.
     12 Guns of different sizes,
     50 European artillery, and Basalet Jung has 4,700 horse and some sepoys at Adoni.

Lally was encamped near Adoni the 12th instant, and preparing to march towards the Kistna. He applied to Basalet Jung (in consequence of a letter from Mr. Bellecombe) for permission to assist the French. The answer that was given is not perfectly known, but it is confidently said, that he will be soon this way. Twenty cofs north of Ongole is a party of five hundred sepoys, and a company of Europeans, with some guns, under the command of a Frenchman named Hornet.

My force, although weak, must be divided for the security of a great extent of country. I judged it necessary to send seven companies of sepoys, under captain Bridges, south of the Kistna, to watch the motions of Mr. Hornet, to protect that part of our Circar, and to prevent the embarking of troops for Pondicherry, or landing of any to reinforce Mr. Lally. They will also attend to Lally, should he move down, and be ready to retard his going towards you, sir, should he be so inclined. Proper directions are given to captain Bridges to secure a timely retreat.

I have encamped within four miles of Masulipatam five hundred men of captain Johnstone's battalion ready to support any part threatened. Part of captain Powell's battalion with four six pounders will join me in a few days; which, with captain Johnstone's and those under captain Bridges, will not amount to twelve hundred effective men.

It being thought necessary to secure the late conquest of Yanam, a company is ordered there; and a hill Rajah who threatens conflagration to some villages north of Samulcotah, obliges me to send one hundred men to protect that part. So you, sir, will perceive that I have a great deal to do with a small force.

Samulcotah and Ellore are evacuated: the artillery and stores are ordered to Masulipatam.

The fortress of Condapilly is in such a condition as to be incapable of defence, excepting there was a garrison of 3000 men. Of the gun carriages only two can be removed without dissolution; they will not bear many discharges, and not one besides these can support a gun.

As I can only spare two hundred men for this place, I have abandoned all the hills, excepting what these two hundred men may defend against an army; and I shall, if the chief and council permits me, send carriages to mount what guns are necessary.

I have the honour to be, &c.

Richard Mathews.

Camp, *Aug.* 29, 1778.

Major

Major Mathews, to the Hon. Thomas Rumbold, Esq; President, &c.

Honourable Sir,

Some days ago I was informed by the chief and council, that Rajanah Dourah of Tontapilly was raising men with an intention of committing ravages on the territories of Reddapore, Pettipore, and Samulcotah, whose inhabitants were greatly alarmed, because the garrison of Samulcotah was to be witdrawn. Some time after the chief and council wrote to me that captain Powell had in his possession, as prisoners, the father of the above Rajanah Dourah, and four others, also a woman, and desired me to give orders to captain Powell concerning them. I directed captain Powell to bring them August 25. here, and wrote to Rajanah Dourah to discharge his levies, August 25. and wait the justice of the new chief, Mr. Cotsford, who I made no doubt would release his father.

Upon captain Powell's arrival I found that Yencanah Dourah* had been in confinement twelve months, was very old, and could not be if enlarged of any disservice, or, as a prisoner, of any service to the honourable company; whereas if he had his liberty it might induce his son to be quiet and leave his claims on the Tontapilly country to your decision, which at this time would be a great point gained by enabling me to draw to the Kistna that force which must otherwise be kept for the security of Peddapore, &c.

Ra-

---

* Captain Powell to Major Matthews.

The following is, to the best of my recollection, the purport of conversation, between Major Mathews, and Yencanah Dourah, the 2d of September, at Gundoor, where the Major released him.

Major Mathews informed him Yencanah Dourah, through Langum Dourah his Dubash, that if he would promise to return immediately home, and there remain quiet, and not interfere in any shape with the management of the country, and oblige his son Rajanah Dourah to discharge his Peons, and other fighting people, and do the same,

[36]

Rajanah Dourah was lately under the protection of Viziaramrauze, was with him and our troops during the late troubles near Madagoil, and receives (it is said) affiftance in his levies from that diftrict.

Sept. 2.

To obviate the aforementioned difficulties, I have releafed Yencanah Dourah, making him promife to perfuade his fon to give us no trouble.

I have reafon to think that if I had propofed the meafure to the chief and council, they would have objected to it; and probably might have referred it to the honourable felect committee, if the honourable felect committee had previoufly known of the man's confinement. A fortnight or more would have been taken up in determining the point, in which time Rajanah Dourah would have begun his devaftations, and part of my fmall force called away. Whereas by the ftep that I have prefumed to take, thefe impediments to the public fervice are avoided; and I beg, fir, that you will believe I had nothing elfe in view.

By the general orders of the 12th ult. Jamadars, Havaldars, Naikes, and fepoys are, from different battalions, to be promoted for thofe to be raifed. I muft requeft that you will permit me to defer the promotion until the battallions, or, at leaft, fome number of

fame, he would releafe him; the Major further told him, by fuch behaviour his fon might, perhaps, get poffeffion of his country again; but that if either he, his fon, or any of the family, fhould offer to commit any depredations in any part of the country belonging to the Honourable Company, fhould he, or they, be taken, they muft expect no mercy.

Yencanah Dourah then gave Major Mathews, in writing, a promife of his good behaviour; at which time the Major delivered to him a fmall box of gold and filver jewels, and two croffes, which were found with him when he was taken by lieutenant M'Gill. Major Mathews directed me to give from my battalion, a Naigue and four fepoys, as an efcort, to fee him as far as he chofe on his way homeward.

James Powell.

Ellore, October 10, 1778.

of men are collected; that those who exert themselves in recruiting, and are otherwise worthy of promotion may receive the reward due to their merit. Officers commanding the old battalions will not send the best Jemadars, &c. from themselves, and the keeping those sent (for the present) to their old rank will be a saving to the honourable company.

   I am, &c.

             Richard Mathews.

Camp, Sept. 4, 1778.

    Major Mathews, to General Munro.

Sir,

By the General Orders of the 12th of August, Jemadars, Havaldars, Naikes and sepoys are from different batallions to be promoted for those to be raised.

I must beg, sir, that you will permit me to defer this promotion until the battalions, or, at least, some number of either are collected: that those who exert themselves in recruiting, and are otherwise worthy of promotion, may receive the reward due to their merit. Officers commanding the old battalions will not send the best Jemadars, &c. from themselves; and the keeping those sent (for the present) to their old rank will be a saving to the honourable company.

The sepoys of this district have been so much dispersed that the battalions are not in very good order, although by no means the fault of the officers, who are as capable as any in the service. The battalions have also a number of recruits which makes the field-return very weak. Many sepoys have been, and still are, singly in different villages that do not chose to come in. Enjoying full pay and batta they are satisfied with a life of idleness, that renders them no better than recruits, when they rejoin their battalion. But several judge it to be more advantageous to desert with their arms, than to renew the toil of learning to handle them adroitly.

Dubashes and others (not officers) find their account in employing sepoys to force the inhabitants to pay money. For the poor farmers are obliged to pay a quarter of a rupee batta *per* day for each private sepoy; which sepoy thinks himself well rewarded, for military assistance, if he receives half of it; the person who employs him gets the other half. This is one source of disorder and general complaint of imposition in this Circar.

I beg leave to recommend that the battalions in this district be reformed to 750 men each, to consist of only five companies. If this took place through the service, there would be a saving to the honourable company of forty thousand pagodas *per annum*. The number of Subadars, Jemadars, Havaldars, and Naikes would be less, of sepoys more; and the battalions would be at all times fitter for action. Each company will be a grand division capable of acting independently; the manœuvres to be the same as hitherto; the firing different, which will be as the old Duke of Cumberland directed, by distinct grand divisions, the only way to throw in the greatest fire without confusion to the general arrangement. I hope that you will have no objection to my practising this method, the success of which I will answer for.

There are in the different batallions several men who through length of service are unfit for the field. These may, if you please, be formed into a company for garrison duty at Masulipatam.

I have the honour, &c.

Richard Mathews.

Camp, Sept. 4, 1778.

Major

Major Mathews, to General Munro.

Sir,

The inclosed orders that I lately gave to captain James Powell will shew you my intentions in having a good party south of the Kistna; it not only serving to protect our own country, but keeps Basalet Jung in awe for fear of Guntoor, and forces him to prevent Lally's acting in support of his countrymen. It is my opinion that we should *this way* wear the appearances of not being weak, in order to imprefs our neighbours with an idea of our strength arising from confidence in ourselves. It was with this view as well as the real one of impeding the march of Lally and of Basalet Jung's troops, who might (for what I know to the contrary) move to the southward to make a diversion in favour of the French, that I have acted as my public orders will shew. But I am now sorry to inform you, that it is out of my power to continue the same plan; and Lally with his troops and Basalet Jung's cavalry may march with impunity to the southward, as I have received orders not to move any troops towards Basalet Jung's country, and in consequence to withdraw the detachment that is now over the Kistna.

The river Kistna, to within a few miles of the sea, divides the Guntoor Circar from the major part of our lands; but we have a considerable portion on the south side called the Nigampatam Circar. Our troops to get to that Circar must pass through part of Basalet Jung's, and then, from the narrow limits of our land, be almost close to Basalet Jung's territory.

I have been compelled, against my own judgment, to recall those troops that were stationed for the purposes before-mentioned; and I request, sir, that you will from this time not blame me for any accident that happens south of the Kistna that may affect your operations, or, the present security of the Carnatic.

Between me and the company's country, south of the Kistna, will be a navigable river three quarters of a mile in breadth, not fordable for many leagues inland until the month of February. You, sir, must know, that to force a passage in the face of an enemy, will require a great superiority of troops; also a great number of boats to transport them, neither of these are in this Circar. The chief and council objected to five boats that I have detained; these five will not convey two three pounders and four companies of sepoys across in less than two days. Judge then how long it would take to pass such a detachment as would be proper to follow Lally close. This Frenchman may now with a small force take possession of the banks of the river, and do what he pleases to the southward; for it will be madness to attempt a passage in the face of an enemy that is much superior, who knows how to act.

By the representation of the chief and council of Masulipatam, I am apprehensive of being hurt in the opinion of the honourable select committee; am lately forbid to correspond with the select committee, and by them directed to "obey implicitly" the requisitions I may receive from the chief and council. How far this may be conformable to the spirit and intentions of the honourable the court of Directors, I shall leave to the decision of my superiors, being willing at this time of general danger to do my utmost to prove myself a faithful servant to the company.

As it is my duty to inform you of military occurrences, I may reasonably expect to find in you, my commander in chief, a steady assertor of military rights.

I cannot help saying, that I am afraid that the colourings of the chief and council have concealed the truth; or else I should not be so severely condemned on the head of disrespect to Mr. Sadleir and council. I shall take the liberty of laying the matter before you so far, as what I suppose is the cause of the dispute; not with a view to ac-

quire

quire an improper authority, but to be enabled to do justice to my employers, and to expose duplicity.

I have to request that you will make all, or, what part of this letter you think proper, known to the honourable select committee; that they may see my true reasons for sending a detachment over the Kistna, and this should be done speedily to avoid bad consequences that may ensue from having no troops south of the Kistna; or, near the sea-ports belonging to Basalet Jung. A respectable party should be there for the aforementioned reasons, and not a small number who daily run the risque of being demolished.

I take the liberty of inclosing the orders that I gave to the detachments over the river, which I hope will meet with your approbation. I am also under the necessity of transmitting you an order[*] that I thought proper to issue to every battalion in this district; which order Mr. Sadleir would not, for some time, permit to be published to captain Rowles's battalion, and thereby occasioned the correspondence which you will herewith receive.

I gave orders about the Lascars, when the French squadron was expected at Masulipatam or Coringy. It was then necessary to make some

---

[*] Copy of Orders issued by Major Matthews, Sept. 3, 1778, respecting Absentees.

Camp at Gundoor, Thursday Sept. 3, 1778.

The number of sepoys that are absent from their battalions, on pretence of revenue service, many of whom cannot be heard of, and others have the assurance to send excuses for not coming in according to orders,—That these men may in future have no plea or advantage from the Hon. Company, by staying from their duty, they will after this month be struck off the rolls, and considered as deserters; their pay will also be detained in the hands of the Paymaster, who will not issue it to those who may return from such commands, unless they bring a note from the commanding officer of the battalion.

Captains of battalions will be pleased to make this as public as possible, that their Absentees may immediately join them.

Richard Matthews.

some alteration of the artillery that were planted improperly on the walls, and Lascars could not be procured for that purpose; at the same time, I saw that an improper use was made of them by some gentlemen of the civil line.

    I have the honour, &c.

              Richard Mathews.

Camp, Sept. 12, 1778.

    Major Mathews, to General Munro.

Sir,

  I have just now received information that Mr. Lally with all his force, and the greatest part of Basalet Jung's cavalry, have left Adoni, and marched to the southward; it was reported, to compel a dependent Rajah to pay the usual tribute. What may be their real intentions I know not; but whatever comes to my knowledge, you shall be acquainted with.

    I have the honour, &c.

              Richard Mathews.

Camp, Sept. 20, 1778.

    Major Mathews, to General Munro.

Sir,

  In the letter that I had the honour of addressing you the 12th inst. I promised to lay before you the cause of the disputes between the chief and council and me.

  The accompanying extracts of a letter from the honourable select committee, with my replies, will in a small degree shew you, why the chief and council are determined not to agree with me.

  Before my arrival in this district the several officers were kept independent of each other. Divide to rule, has been the maxim of
                      the

the chiefs and council for some years; this fully answers their own purposes. The senior officer in the district had no more authority in point of command than the youngest when detached; and the honourable company's regulations in this respect has been totally neglected, very much to the detriment of the service.

As I had orders to collect the troops for the defence of the district, and was expresly appointed to command them, as the inclosed letter, (see p. 11.) from the honourable select committee, dated the 7th of August, will shew.

I required upon my first arrival that the chief and council would acquaint the several independent commanding officers that in future they were to obey me. This the chief and council wished to evade, and did so, by issuing directions only, that my appointment should be made public in the " usual form and manner." What they meant was very clear, because it had been usual for the senior officer not to have any superior military authority: he was as low as any, that were favoured with a separate command. And this their meaning was further proved by their sending orders for removals, and relieving troops to several commanding officers after my arrival. If I had not remonstrated against this breach of the public regulations, and asserted the rights of the military in that of my own, you, sir, in particular, and all my brother officers would have uniformly condemned me for betraying, at this time, the sacred cause of the defenders of the company's possessions. For the point once given up is with difficulty recovered; so it has happened in this district.

I have to request of you, sir, to prevent my being given up to civil lust of unnatural power: and that in the present instance I may have fair-play. I have already been forced to make my defence from the sentences of condemnation, which is altogether new in civil and military law.

Be pleased to let me be favoured with copies of all letters that the chief and council have wrote concerning me; that my defence may be made so as to convince you and the honourable select committee, that my disposition is not for disputation: but that I am zealous for the cause of my employers the honourable company, and for the just rights of the military who have in these Circars been shamefully depressed.

The remains of eight companies of captain Lane's battalion arrived in this district a few days ago from Vizagapatam. It is so much reduced by sickness and desertion that, exclusive of recruits, I could scarcely select two complete companies fit for duty out of the eight.

I have the honour to be, &c.

Richard Mathews.

Camp, Sept. 21, 1778.

Extracts of a Letter from the honourable Select Committee to Major Mathews, dated Sept. 6, 1778, *with Major Mathews's Defence, sent to General Munro, Sept.* 21, 1778.

Ext. 1. We intended that the chief and council should follow your recommendation and opinion in respect to the arrangement of the troops for the security of the district; but we meant also that you should pay a proper regard to their sentiments and advice, which you appear not to have done.

Def. 1. It is impossible to observe such a line of conduct at present, as the honourable select committee mentions; for if the sentiments of the military officer, and those of the chief and council differ, it does not determine which shall be followed. If the arrangement of the troops for the security of the district is left to the judgment of the military, the officer will pursue such a plan as experience

perience suggests. If this arrangement be left to the chief and council, whose ideas from want of the necessary military knowledge must differ from those who are educated in the field; they will follow notions that may be the reverse to true ones. Their sentiments and advice may enlarge the ideas of an officer, but the real executive part should be left to him.

Ext. 2. We are sorry to remark a want of respect on your part, in declining to attend their board when desired to do so. The reasons assigned by you on this occasion are not satisfactory.

Def. 2. I cannot accuse myself for want of respect to the board of Masulipatam. They from the first seemed determined to throw every obstacle in the way to my having the command of the troops, and to the drawing them from their former stations. They were not ignorant of my orders, nor the views of the honourable select committee. Mr. Sadleir had conversed with me often upon the subject. The last time was in the morning that he asked me to attend the board. I could not say any more on the topic than what had been repeated many times, and it appearing that the board wanted to evade complying with the orders of the honourable select committee, I declined going, and desired Mr. Sadleir to inform the board of my sentiments, which he promised to do. I cannot think that in this conduct of mine I was guilty of any disrespect. They had positive and plain orders, which they wished to evade: I was endeavouring to act in the strictest conformity to the orders I received from the honourable the select committee.

Ext. 3. In regard to the requisitions for troops which were sent from the chief and council a few days after your arrival, without being communicated to you, we have expressed to them our opinion that they acted improperly; but at the same time, we cannot pass unnoticed the disrespectful style of your letter to them in consequence, wherein you speak of that proceeding in terms very reprehensible.

Def.

Def. 3. The style of my letter was to set forth the inconsistency of their conduct in endeavouring by all means to overset, and render of no effect, the orders of the honourable select committee. When men sink beneath the dignity of station they are not entitled to respect.

Ext. 4. Withdrawing the sepoys employed on the revenue service, disrespectful and unauthorised.

Def. 4. Withdrawing the sepoys that were dispersed, not only all over our Circars, but in the Guntoor Circar, and towards Hydrabad, on pretence of revenue service, was acting in conformity to the orders of the honourable select committee, which were, to collect the troops for the defence of the district, and in this respect I I hope that my conduct will appear more deserving of applause than censure.

Ext. 5. Your ordering the delivery and removal of stores from Ellore without authority from them (the chief and council) disrespectful and unauthorised.

Def. 5. The removal of the stores from Ellore has not been truly explained. The garrisons of Samulcotah and Ellore were ordered to be instantly evacuated. The stores were immediately to be removed according to the arrangement that I sent to the chief and council on the 15th of August. There were some reasons to expect that the country would be invaded (that it has not is no proof to the contrary). The stores if left at Ellore were without protection; besides it was attended with unnecessary expence to the company; and as the chief and council did not give any directions for their removal, I issued the necessary orders to the officer on the 18th of August, and acquainted the storekeeper of it. I had in view to secure the stores, and ordered some to Masulipatam, some to Condapilly, and some for the use the troops in the field. But upon my visiting

the

the fortress of Condapilly* I found it in such a condition that I did not think it a secure place for the stores, so sent them to Masulipatam.

Whenever I wanted stores I have indented to the chief and council for them. They cannot say otherwise. But in the above instance it was the removal of the stores from an improper situation to a secure one, immediately under the eye of the chief and council; and in so doing I flattered myself that I was performing my duty.

Ext. 6. With respect to the Lascars of the garrison, without considering or writing to them on the subject, disrespectful and unauthorised.

Def. 6. I received a letter from the honourable select committee dated the 22d of August, informing me, that the French squadron had escaped from Sir Edward Vernon, and might probably come to the northward, desiring me to pay the utmost attention to secure Masulipatam and the port of Coringy. (see p. 13.) At this time in the fort of Masulipatam there were very few Europeans: but by report I heard there were near two hundred good Lascars. It was necessary to place the artillery on the walls where they would be of service, and to have people ready, at night especially, to work them. Not one of the Lascars was under the authority of the commanding officer, but they were variously employed by the civil gentlemen.

When a garrison is attacked, the lot falls upon the military to defend the place. And having only (according to the present system) the power of acting upon the appearance of an enemy, he is, in fact, taken by surprise, and may, in an instant, lose his good name. That things might be put into some order, to prevent danger, I desired

---

* This fortress in ruins, but a large sum of money had been charged the company for erecting barracks for officers and sepoys in a useless and unhealthy situation at the foot of the rock.

fired captain Rowles to apply for Lafcars. He was always refufed. But upon the receipt of the aforementioned orders from the honourable felect committee, I directed captain Rowles to learn the number of Lafcars that were in garrifon: becaufe if he fhould be attacked, he had only thofe to depend upon for managing the artillery. He was anfwered by Mr. Sadleir in an uncivil manner, and not a military one: and could not get a man to enable him to obey my orders for to put the fort in a proper ftate of defence.

I did not perceive any neceffity of lofing fo much time as to write to the chief and council about the Lafcars: and the event is fufficient to fhew that fuch application would have no effect.

Ext. 7. Omitting to furnifh them (the chief and council) with advice concerning your operations until they had been in part executed, whereby they were deprived of the opportunity of giving you their fentiments in time upon fuch points as might require them; difrefpectful and unauthorifed.

Def. 7. No operations worth notice have taken place without advifing the chief and council of them. But as the defence of the diftrict was left to me, and the conduct of the chief and council appeared to run counter to every propofal that I made, I did not think it neceffary to obtain their confent, or wait their orders for the movement of troops over the Kiftna; the only circumftance in which I may be thought blameable. But the difpofition has been honoured by the approval of the commander in chief.

Ext. 8. The chief and council are the perfons charged under us, with the interefts and affairs of the company in the Circars. They are left to be the judges when military affiftance is neceffary for the purpofes of revenue, or, on any other fervice, and are empowered to make requifitions which on the part of the commanding officer are to receive implicit obedience.

Def.

Def. 8. This a point that may be easily settled. Is the defence of the district left to the judgment of the military, or not? By the regulations from Europe it is: also, by the practice in the subordinates at Bengal, according to the sentiments of General Clavering; and it was left to me by the orders that I had the honour of receiving from the honourable the select committee. The interests and affairs of the company of a civil nature, and of revenue are the province of the chief and council. The military commanding officer is to assist them, when they require it, the service to be performed being made known.

But I conceive that, in respect to stationing troops, occasionally removing them, and all military and regimental discipline and detail, the chief and council have no concern with.

Ext. 9. It was not within your province to determine whether the troops, which had been required and employed on the revenue service, were necessary or might be recalled; much less was it so to proceed to the actual recall of them without any authority whatever, and without knowing what detriment it might cause to the collections.

Def. 9. Answered by the foregoing; and the 4th paragraph excepting the recall, which was in consequence of my orders from the honourable select committee, and the abuse made of those reported on revenue service.

Ext. 10. The arrangement and issues of stores also compose a part of the duty of the chief and council, and not a single article is permitted to be delivered for use, or removed from place to place without their express orders. We are surprised that this circumstance should have been unknown to you, or that you should have disregarded it in the manner you appear to have done. In future no stores are to be delivered to you without a regular indent to the chief and council, or removed from place to place without their authority.

Def. 10. The military regulations have made me acquainted with the mode of application for stores which I have observed.

Ext. 11. In respect to the letter addressed by captain Rowles to the chief and council of Masulipatam, in consequence of your orders; the manner of this proceeding is on your part disrespectful. The Lascars are entirely under the direction of the chief and council; you ordering captain Rowles to consider them as part of the strength of the garrison, and to require an account of their number, how employed, &c. without previously consulting with the chief and council here, or desiring their permission to include them in the strength of the garrison, was evidently passing beyond the bounds of your authority at the same time it was disrespectful.

Def. 11. The reason for requiring a knowledge of the number of Lascars has been mentioned in the 6th paragraph. The fort was to be secured from surprise, and put into a state of defence. And this was in consequence of the orders of the honourable select committee, and of hourly expecting the French fleet. When the enemy are before the place, it is certain that the chief and council can have nothing to do with the Lascars, or with any part of the garrison.

Major Mathews, to General Munro.

Sir,

I have the honour to transmit to you the monthly returns, with returns of casualties from the 29th of June to the end of September; also field returns of the battalions at Ellore *(see Appendix)*, by which you will perceive that the real strength of each of them for action doth not amount to four hundred firelocks, including a select
picquet

picquet that is near our frontier. The rolls of the battalions are swelled by recruits;—sick, and absent on revenue business, who are of no immediate service to us. We now want to complete the battalions in this district six hundred and nineteen men. Since the order came to raise the new battalions we have not been able to recruit more than three hundred men, which are too few to complete the old battalions; and presents us with a poor prospect of increasing the force in this Circar by new levies.

Our neighbours are preparing for war, and have for a long time been employed in raising men, which is an impediment to our recruiting views; for idle men wish to serve those that give least trouble, and where discipline and subordination are too weak to enforce obedience.

In my letter of the 4th of September I requested permission to defer the promotion of the Jemadars, Havaldars, Naikes, and sepoys that were sent from the old battalions for the new; as it would be a saving to the company, and afford an opportunity to reward merit that might shew itself in procuring recruits, and forming them for service. Several of different ranks that have been sent seem to me unfit for higher trust. The little success that we have met with in the recruiting business will be an apology for my keeping the aforementioned people to their old rank; because if any other plan should be adopted it will not, on this account, be attended with an additional expence to the company, by having supernumerary Indian commissioned and non-commissioned officers.

Captain Charles Frazer is arrived at Masulipatam, with about sixty recruits. Captain Nixon, by the assistance of the men from other battalions, has collected about two hundred and forty, which, with those of captain Frazer's, I have put under the charge of lieutenant Moslay, who is a good officer, and every way capable of instructing them. He was many years adjutant to the second battalion, and understands the country language sufficient to explain what is proper for sepoys to be taught.

I am much concerned to tell you, that I think it impossible to raise a new battalion in twelve months. The honourable select committee were made acquainted with this opinion of mine on the 20th of August.

The weakness of the two battalions at Ellore, induced me to throw two companies into one, that officers may be with each company, and be better known to the men. It makes no difference on the general roll of the battalion, or of the payments; and I only mention it, as without an explanation it might appear a reform that decreased the fixed establishment.

The first Circar battalion was diminished the last month by desertion, &c. one hundred and forty men; and the real strength of the other battalions will not enable me to draw together fit for action in the field above twelve hundred firelocks: too small a number to oppose a powerful invasion.

In a former letter I took the liberty of mentioning a reform of the battalions of this Circar into five companies, and that it would be attended with great advantages to the service; particularly at this time, that we are to depend, in a very considerable degree, upon them, having but few European infantry for such an extensive territory. Inclosed is a return of the state of a battalion of five companies. By this plan you, sir, will be enabled to promote many deserving lieutenants that have been from nine to twelve years in the service. And by the number of European officers to each battalion add much weight to our mercenaries, as well as a firmer check upon their behaviour.

By the last accounts Mr. Lally was at Adoni.

Two

Two Zemindars of the Guntoor Circar have assembled at Innacundah, about two days journey from Ongole, 4000 sepoys and Peons, 300 Arabs, a few horse, and some small guns, who give out that they intend to attack Monickrow, who is tributary to Basalat Jung. But by their going so far to the southward, I apprehend that they there wait for the event of the siege of Pondicherry, being prepared to act against us if a good opportunity offers. If a respectable detachment had continued to the southward of the Kistna, these people would not have dared to assemble. Inacundah is on the high road from Adoni to Guntoor, and it is reported that Mr. Lally will join the party at that place in a few days.

I have at different times received so many contradictory reports of Lally's motions, that I am unwilling to say any thing about him; but the troops said to be at Inacundah, are certainly there. The Zemindar* at the head of the party is tributary to us for lands that he has to the northward of the Kistna.

The managers for Narsiah, another tributary of ours, a few days ago entered into a treaty with Manickrow, and promised to assist him immediately with one thousand men; and after the rains, with another thousand, and one or two guns. As soon as these circumstances came to my knowledge, I sent an officer and sixty men to compel our tributary to discharge his levies; and to order him to desist from sending any armed men across the Kistna, as it might involve us in a dispute with Basalat Jung: a circumstance that should be avoided at this particular time. The appearance of the officer and sepoys had the desired effect, and the tributary has promised not to collect any men without permission of the chief and council.

I am much concerned at being obliged to observe to you, that the inclinations of the natives in this Circar are not in our favour. The warlike preparations of the Soubah may very likely tend this way;
it

* Wassyreddy-ramanah.

it is, therefore, necessary that we should provide for the worst, by establishing without loss of time a sufficient magazine of provisions at Condapilly (the only secure place excepting Masulipatam) from whence the troops in the field may be supplied, as well as a proper store for the consumption of the garrison for at least twelve months. Any quantity of grain might be procured in the Cicacole Circar, and brought in the next month and December to Masulipatam, to the great advantage of the company, because at this time Paddy is at a very low price about Cicacole.

Should this country be invaded, I am persuaded that we should find many enemies in those who now appear friends; and we have not any stock of grain for the support of the troops excepting a small quantity at Condapilly, for four or five hundred men, for two or three months; and what the gentlemen at Masulipatam are laying in to that fort by order of the honourable the select committee. If we wait until the country is invaded I am confident that we shall have to depend upon the stock that will be in Masulipatam.

The inhabitants are much alarmed by travellers, and already talk of a change. Some sepoys belonging to Viziaramrauze have industriously reported that the French will soon have the upper hand in the country, and that our loss before Pondicherry has given the enemy the superiority; although there may not be a word of truth in such stories, yet they have had a bad effect, and I think it my duty to communicate it to you, as well as any other matter that may tend to the preservation of the Circars.

On the 21st of September I troubled you with some papers. The multiplicity of business that you are engaged in has prevented a reply. I must now acquaint you, that Mr. Cotsford thinks that the commanding officer in the district should obey all orders whatever that the chief and council should issue, and be entirely under them. I have done myself the honour of informing you of my opinion of

the

the sense of the regulations from Europe, and have been favoured with your construction of a most material article, which shall be the rule of my conduct; for though as an individual I have the highest veneration of Mr. Cotsford's judgment and capacity, and which I would in most things (even in military matters) prefer to my own; yet, as we walk in different lines, I will not let private friendship and esteem betray the rights of my profession. Nor, on the other hand, would I willingly disagree with him. But as he may strenuously assert and endeavour to extend the military authority of the chief and council being supported by the honourable select committee, which authority, if they really have any in military matters, I conceive to be ill placed in a chief and council; the council being for the most part young men totally uninformed and unacquainted with military affairs; and who from pride of local station do not at all times behave with proper attention to officers. I therefore, rather than be thought litigious, will, though with concern, especially as the time is approaching that requires every possible exertion to save our possessions, suffer a removal if it be your pleasure. I have heard that the governor has threatened to remove me because I made known my complaints,* where I have every reason to expect redress. I therefore beg leave to repeat that I am resolved to act for the benefit of the Honourable Company, according as I think was the intentions of the Court of Directors, by the standing orders that they sent to India: wherein they drew the line between the civil and military powers; and shall wait with all due submission for your commands, and for those of the honourable select committee. In the mean time I shall enforce the following orders to all officers in this district.

" All officers that are detached are to comply with every requi-
" sition that the chief and council of Masulipatam may make agree-
" ably to the honourable company's regulation to support their civil
" jurisdiction, or for the purposes of revenue. But on all oc-
" currences

* To the commander in chief.

" rences that are purely military, he will only obey the orders of
" the honourable select committee, the commander in chief of the
" forces, or, the commanding officer of the troops in the district,
" according to the rules of the army."

The above is strictly conformable to my opinion that the defence of the district should be vested in the military commanding officer, who should not be controuled by the chief and council in respect to the motion or discipline of the troops.

Some days ago I wrote to captain Bridges to send me up two men to assist in drilling the recruits; but the chief and council of Masulipatam will not permit captain Bridges to send them. You will herewith receive copies of letters that passed upon this occasion.

The honourable select committee have thought proper to send orders, *"That no garrison order whatever shall be issued in the fort of
" Masulipatam without the sanction of the chief and council."

Which

---

* The garrison order concerning sepoys employed on revenue service, issued by order of Major Mathews, from Gundoor, the 3d, and in this garrison by captain Rowles the 6th instant, without the concurrence of the chief and council, being judged by them an unwarrantable proceeding, It has been referred to the honourable the President and select committee of Fort St. George, who have been pleased to express their sense of it as follows. Extracted from their letter, dated the 11th instant.

We much disapprove of the order being issued in your garrison, without your consent, and direct that in future no garrison order whatsoever be published until it has received your sanction.

By order of the chief and council,
Signed   *Thomas Barnard*, Secretary.
Masulipatam, Sept. 24, 1778.   A true Copy.

The chief and council, with their usual art, were willing to take advantage of this order to seize the small remains of military authority, even so low as to regimental duty and detail; for instead of issuing the order in the exact words of the select committee, they thought it more convenient to promulge, " that no order whatever should
" be issued without their sanction." The select committee directed, " that no gar-
" rison order should be issued without the sanction of the chief and council.

Which order is so general that I am at a loss how to give any order concerning discipline or detail to the officer commanding the troops; because he may disobey me and shelter himself under the general order, by an application to the chief and council, who by the regulations have nothing to do with military detail.

You will perceive that the chief and council have much at heart the preservation and security of Masulipatam, by the stress they lay in, and dependence they put upon an invalid corporal, as (they say) " his absence would weaken the garrison."

I have the honour, &c.

Richard Mathews.

Ellore, Oct. 22, 1778.

Major Mathews, to the Hon. Thomas Rumbold, Esq;

Honourable Sir,

I take the liberty of sending you extracts of a letter that I wrote this day to General Munro, that you may judge how far it is possible to raise the two battalions that were ordered by the honourable select committee. The inclosed returns of casualties will make the matter clear to you.

I have also transmitted a state of a battalion, such as, I think, would answer well for the Circars, and for the establishment in general; and what may be particularly necessary at this time, when we are forced to place so much dependence upon mercenaries.

I flatter myself that I am doing my duty, when I attempt to benefit the service; and shall not be chagrined at the rejection of my proposal.

I have the honour, &c.

Richard Mathews.

Ellore, Oct. 22, 1778.

Major Mathews, to General Munro.

Sir,

This morning I received the inclosed.* The attack is so pointed that I have been forced to make a reply as will sufficiently explain the part I mean to act. Copy thereof accompanies this.

You, sir, will perceive that the chief and council have it in view to sink the commanding officer of the troops into a mere Roster-keeper; defining away all the honourable part of his military authority, and leaving him the clerk-like occupation of keeping the detail only.

I have to request once more your interposition, that I may be enabled to do my duty to the honourable company, free from such embarassments as able penmen are capable of throwing in the way of a soldier.

I have the honour to be, &c.

Ellore, Oct. 23, 1778.

Richard Mathews.

Major Mathews, to General Munro.

Sir,

Permit me to present my respectful congratulations upon your success against Pondicherry. It is an event that secures the peace of the Carnatic, and decides in our favour the voices of our neighbours, who might have been emboldened to break with us upon an expectation of support from the French, who have no longer power to injure us on the coast.

The inclosed extract will shew you that I am in a manner baited. A wrong construction seems to be put upon every act.

I am

---

* A letter from the chief and council.

I am sorry to trouble you; but to whom can I apply so properly as to the head of the military; especially as a direct intercourse with the honourable select committee is forbidden.

The representations of the chief and council goes in a flowing robe, which may be tinged with part of my colours and substance, but, in fact, leaves me bare in the article of vindication. The accompanying letter is my last to them. I wish most sincerely that it may be the last I shall have occasion to write in such a style.

I have the honour, &c.

Richard Mathews.

Ellore, Oct. 26, 1778.

Major Mathews, to the Hon. Thomas Rumbold, Esq; Governor, &c. and Select Committee.

Honourable Sir, and Sirs,

Lieutenant Abbot has informed you that a ship, supposed to be French, was seen off Mutapilly,* the sea-port near to Yentapollam, and that it was supposed she had on board two hundred soldiers; which information induced me to come thus far. The defenceless state of this part of the coast occasioned captain Barclay to reinforce Mr. Abbot with a company of sepoys, and to have another in the way to join him, should there appear a necessity of collecting more force. And truly should the French think seriously of landing hereabout, and Basalat Jung determine to support, or, rather to receive succour from them, the small party that are on this side of the Kistna cannot frustrate their intentions. I could wish that, at least, a battalion were stationed for this purpose.

I have this morning been several miles along the beach; not a vessel to be seen: those that were in sight yesterday are sailed to the

* A sea-port belonging to Basalat Jung.

northward. The surf near Mutapilly is in general so low that pinnaces or jolly-boats can come through it without any risque.

I have the honour, &c.

Tentapollam, Nov. 16, 1778.

Richard Mathews.

Major Mathews, to the Hon. Thomas Rumbold, Esq; Governor, &c. and Select Committee.

Honourable Sir, and Sirs,

Lieutenant Abbot has informed you that Monf. Bon-enfant landed some days ago near this place, and had the protection of the Guntoor Circar. This morning I received a letter from Munagulla, a place ten cofs from Cambamet, acquainting me of his having passed through that place on his way to Hydrabad; and that he had with him twenty sepoys as an escort.

We have not seen any vessel this day.

I have the honour to be, &c.

Tentapollam, Nov. 17, 1778.

Richard Mathews.

Major Mathews, to the Hon. Thomas Rumbold, Esq; Governor, &c. and Select Committee.

Honourable Sir, and Sirs,

The day before yesterday a party of sepoys met with a Frenchman and brought him hither. He says, that he served a gentleman now in the Guntoor Circar, and was, when seized, on his way to this place, from whence he purposed going to Pulicat. He gave in writing a state of the troops with Basalat Jung; particularly of Lally's

*Lally's party, which he deſcribes as very formidable; as it is badly wrote and I cannot tranſlate it I have forwarded it to Mr. Henry Caſamaijor, that a fair copy may be preſented to you. I have ſent the man to Ongole, not only for ſecurity, but to enable captain Barclay to

---

* Tranſlation of Intelligence received by a Frenchman, Nov. 19, 1778.

Mr. de Lally's army or party is compoſed of 4000 men, including 500 Europeans. Among this number are 120 well-diſciplined cavalry, which are reckoned the beſt; beſides 3,500 ſepoys, in which are included 500 Topaſſes well-diſciplined. It is from theſe Topaſſes the artillery is ſupplied, conſiderable enough in field-pieces, but inſufficient in battering cannon; beſides there is abſolutely but one officer capable of conducting it.

The following is the rank of officers.

Mr. Lally, General not only of his own party, but likewiſe of the Nabob's party, who can without any difficulty join to the troops of this general 10,000 men, equal in cavalry and infantry, they reckon 2000 black cavalry.

Mr. Le Beuf, commandant.
Mr. Renard, captain major.
Mr. Maugin, captain of his cavalry.
Mr. Berri, captain of infantry and his aid major.
Mr. Collin, lieutenant of cavalry.
Mr. Hornot, lieutenant of infantry, who has been long detached in this province, to overlook the funds deſtined by the Nabob for the payment of the troops of his party.
Mr. Montangon, lieutenant.
Mr. Rainboter, captain of infantry.
Mr. François, lieutenant.
Mr. Pricuré, captain.
Mr. Aidmont, lieutenant.
Mr. Pricuré, who I have already mentioned, conducts the artillery.

The ſepoys of this party are commanded by Europeans, each company conſiſts of 100 men, conducted by a ſerjeant and corporal, independent of the black officers and corporals. Among others, Mr. Lally has joined to his army 200 black cavalry, which belong to the Nabob, well-diſciplined, and much eſteemed. His European infantry, for the moſt part, conſiſts of men who have already ſerved. This general is much reſpected by his troops, and eſteemed by the Nabob; he is a man who is more anxious for a name than riches. Among ſeveral regulations, he diſmiſſes from his party every ſoldier who attempts to take up a ſabre or ſword.

to give your honours any information that the prisoner may have it in his power to disclose worthy your knowledge.

The Zemindars in the Guntoor Circar are in arms, in two parties; whether they mean to attack each other, or to wait the chapter of accidents, is uncertain. The forts of Innacundah and Condaveredurgum are each about sixteen cofs from hence, both on high rocks and well fortified; the latter is at present slightly guarded; the former has a strong garrison; and is on the high road to Adoni, where Mr. Lally is.

I have the honour, &c.

Richard Mathews.

Tentapollam, Nov. 21, 1778.

Major Mathews, to General Munro.

Sir,

By your orders under date the 13th instant, the battalion raising for captain Frazer is to be disbanded, and the men and black officers to be incorporated into captain Nixon's battalion: also that 275 men from other battalions are to join captain Nixon, which together will increase the number of private of the now 9th battalion to double the number as ordered by the last general orders that a battalion should consist of. When the last monthly returns were sent, the aforementioned new battalions were forming very slowly; and whilst Pondicherry was held by our enemies it was difficult to procure recruits; but since the reduction of that fort, many offered their services, indeed more than I had reason to expect, from the backwardness that was evident before that fortunate event. By the weekly returns of the 14th instant, there were at Ellore private sepoys of the 9th battalion 302; and of the 10th 488; exclusive of these there are some with the captains who are at different places recruiting; also many that are with the parties who are employed all over the

district,

diſtrict, and a few in parts adjacent upon the ſame ſervice, which, when they all join at Ellore, to which place I have ordered them all to repair inſtantly, the number of private will amount to more than double what a battalion ſhould conſiſt of.

Although I have not received any orders to ceaſe recruiting, yet, as the battalion that was raiſing is reduced, I am to ſuppoſe that it is only neceſſary to complete the battalions now in being, according to the fixed eſtabliſhment, therefore until further orders I ſhall deſiſt.

The diſtance that my ſituation is from Madras will, in the courſe of a month or ſix weeks, make a very great alteration in reſpect to the number of men reported to you recruited; eſpecially when above twelve parties are employed in different places on the ſame ſervice: this want of information may have occaſioned your ordering ſo many men, more than neceſſary, to complete captain Nixon's battalion.

Your orders will be immediately obeyed; and if there is any error I wait your pleaſure to have it rectified.

As ſoon as captain Nixon, whom I have ordered to Ellore, has formed his battalion, and called in all his out-parties, I will forward a preſent ſtate. In the mean time he will have all thoſe under his charge that you have been pleaſed to direct, agreeably to your orders of the 11th inſtant.

An error that was in the monthly returns for November obliged me to return them to Mr. Schouler, who is ſick at Ellore, or, they would have been forwarded to you before this.

   I have the honour to be, &c.

          Richard Mathews.

Bezoara, Dec. 21, 1778.

              Major

Major Mathews, to General Munro.

Sir,

I have been honoured with your letter concerning captain Bridges. Previous to your order he was directed to proceed to Condapilly, having delivered to captain Long the charge of the troops in Mafulipatam.

I have received the general orders of the 22d ult. *(see p. 5.)* in confequence of which, and as I have not at this time any troops immediately under my command, and my former authority over thofe not prefent ceafing, I have declined acting, and acquainted the chief and council therewith. I requeft of you, fir, that you would be pleafed to permit me to repair to Madras as foon as poffible.

I have the honour, &c.

Richard Mathews.

Mafulipatam, Jan. 2, 1779.

Major Mathews, to Sir Eyre Coote, K. B. Lieutenant-General and Commander in Chief of the forces in India.

Sir,

I take the liberty of congratulating your Excellency on your fafe arrival.

I landed at Madras on the 22d of July, being three months and two days from England. Contrary winds detained me near a month in the Mediterranean, and a revolution at Grand Cairo ftopped me at that place nine days, or my journey would have been, at leaft, as quick as that of Mr. Whitchill's: however, in obfervance to your directions I did not permit "the grafs to grow under my feet." The letter that you honoured me with I delivered; and explained your verbal meffage to General Munro, and to the Nabob.

In consequence of my assertions in England, not to serve under Major Maclellan, I did not go to the siege of Pondicherry; but General Munro will do me the justice to say, that I offered to serve as a volunteer. In the mean time the select committee were very apprehensive of danger to the Circars, from the respectable force that were at that time, and now are under the command of Mr. Lally in the service of Basalat Jung. It was said, that he was then in the Guntoor Circar, which is only separated from the Kistna by this. The rupture with France, our known views towards seizing the Guntoor Circar at the first favourable opportunity, the strength of Lally's party, and our evident weakness in this district, made me conjecture that an active scene of service seemed more than probable. I therefore applied for the command, and had full powers given me in confirmation of the authority vested in the senior military officer by the directions from Europe. This was the immediate source of opposition from the chief and council of this place; who have at length so far prevailed, that the most honourable part of the military power of an officer are totally annihilated, the positive orders of the court of Directors set at nought, and the military prerogative transferred to the gentlemen of the civil line; and in such a manner as to reflect in a great degree upon me in particular, and upon all officers who have served in subordinacies. I have therefore declined acting under the chief and council, and yesterday applied to my then commander in chief for permission to repair to Madras as soon as possible, to which I hope that your Excellency will not have any objections; and that you would be pleased to enable me to pay my respects personally to you before you quit Madras.

   I have the honour, &c.

              Richard Mathews.

Masulipatam, Jan. 3, 1779.

Major Matthews, to Sir Eyre Coote, K. B. Lieutenant-General, &c.

Sir,

Some time before my departure from England I had been solliciting the Court of Directors, with great hopes of success, for my rank above Major Maclellan, who had been placed between Major Charles Hopkins and myself; and when I was desired to carry dispatches of the first importance to India over land, I was promised by the chairman and other gentlemen in the direction, that my rank should be restored to me by the first ship; or, that I should be removed to another establishment, with superior advantages. Neither of these events have taken place; and orders have been received from the India-House without doing honour to those gentlemen who gave me the strongest assurances of justice. Labouring under such a pointed supercession, which is aggravated by something more than the appearance of neglect, I cannot, after having faithfully served the honourable company more than nineteen years, bring my mind to that tranquility as to enable me to wait the arrival of another ship from Europe. When in London, I told the chairman, Mr. Wombwell, that if my rank above Major Maclellan was not sent by the first conveyance, or, a removal from the coast, I should request permission to return immediately to England; to which I hope that your Excellency will not have any objections. I am also induced to go to Europe by the unmerited treatment that I suffered whilst in the district dependent upon Masulipatam.

In my letter of the 3d of January, I took the liberty of mentioning a few circumstances that happened to me after being honoured with the command of the troops in the Masulipatam district. The instant and unremitting opposition that the chief and council made to my exercising the authority that was vested in me, by the standing orders of the Court of Directors, approved and confirmed by a general

neral court of Proprietors, and strengthened by orders from the honourable select committee of Fort St. George, rendered my situation irksome, and my endeavours to correct abuses in some measure ineffectual. But the clear and strongly partial line traced on the 22d of December, has put it out of the power of any military officer (a commanding officer in a district there is not to be) to do, what in such a character is needful for the preservation of the Circars, and to check the rapacity of individuals. Oppression stalks it o'er the land with giant strides.

I was under the necessity of transmitting to the chief and council a petition containing the complaints and grievances of many farmers, who expected that through such a channel they might obtain justice. But instead thereof the chief and council accused me of officiousness, and interfering out of my province. Their unbecoming censure, and the illiberal notice taken of the petition bears the strongest mark that they mean to discourage such instances of zeal in an officer for the welfare of the company; thereby leaving the industrious cultivators of the land to the merciless gripe of renters and their harpies, through all the various modes of extortion.

The chief and council not willing to make any distinction between the commanding officer of the troops in the district, and a Dubash, (so much do they affect impartiality) that they received and countenanced a counter-petition from the Dubash, which, by the falsity of its contents, could be fabricated for no other purpose but to weaken the testimony of those who had complained of his malpractices in his office, as nominal renter of the Ellore Havally.

In a third instance, no notice was taken by the chief and council of a species of tyranny that is too common in the Masulipatam district: of forcing cattle from the inhabitants, on pretence of the company's service, without paying any hire; and pressing men as coolies, without rewarding them for their labour.

The chief and council sent a petition to me, said to have been received by them from the Tanadar of Bezwara, complaining of abuses practised by a detachment stationed at that place. When, after the strictest enquiry, I found that the utmost care had been taken to prevent any cause of complaint, and that the reports were groundless. I have also great reason to believe, that the petition never was sent,*

or

* Translation of a deposition made by Calabarga Juggapau, Tanadar of Bezwara, when he was asked about a complaint preferred by him to the chief and council of Masulipatam.

Beswara, Jan. 1, 1779.

I Calabarga Juggapau, Tanadar of Bezwara, do declare, that I never made any complaint to the chief and council of Masulipatam, against the officers or troops now cantoned at Bezwara; or did they ever give me a cause. I also declare, that the commanding officer there never interfered in the land-customs or any other revenues; or did he, in any manner whatever, prevent me collecting them. I further declare, that no cooleys were ever employed by any of the officers but what were paid by them; and such as were charged for by me, in my accounts, were employed in repairing the Sepoys quarter.

     Signed   *Calabarga Juggapau*, Tanadar of Bezwara.

Witness
Joogia, Conicoply of Bezwara,
Mallia, ditto   ditto,
Amortalingum, Dubash.

Mr. Forbes, to Major Richard Mathews, commanding the troops in the Masulipatam district.

Sir,

I have received your letter of the 21st inst. with Calabarga Juggapau's complaint. I am now to inform you, that the complaints which he has lodged, with regard to land-customs, are groundless. And there is no officer here had occasion for cooleys but Mr. M'Cartey, who got them from the Cutwall, and paid them himself.

Mr. Russell has kept a camp buzar at one end of the village, for the detachment, and supplies it with grain from Ellore; his dubash informs me, that it is brought here without any duties being laid on it.

Accom-

or any complaint made, by the person named as the author of it.

Concerning the glaring and dangerous abuse of employing sepoys, on pretence of revenue service, I have informed General Munro, as also from time to time of the state of the troops. My views have been fixed to the real interest of the honourable company. But the late orders of the 22d of December seem formed to crush the least appearance of public spirit, and to throw obstacles in the way of the officer, to hinder his exertions for the honour and benefit of his country.

I did

Accompanying I return you the letter.
I am, with respect, Sir,
Your most obedient, and most humble servant,

Bezwara, Nov. 24, 1778.
John Forbes.

Mr. James Russell, to Major Richard Mathews, commanding the troops in the Circars.

Sir,

I have the pleasure of your letter of the 21st inst. inclosing a copy of a complaint from Calabarga Juggapau, Tanadar of Bezwara, to the chief and council at Masulipatam, for abuses committed, as he says, by the troops in that cantonment; in answer to which beg leave to declare, that none of them happened, to my knowledge, in the time of my command, and that they are all as infamously false as his barefaced assertion, of not being able to cultivate some fields for want of rain, when it is notorious that all that country has been near covered with water for these six weeks past.

No bramin, or inhabitant whatever were deprived of their houses, or was there any altercation in the arrangement of the officers and Sepoys' quarters, after you left Bezwara, the 26th of August.

I never heard that the sepoys, or others, gave any cause to create confusion in the village, or among the inhabitants; if such had happened, I believe I should be early informed of it, as well as upon one occasion that a sepoy had given offence to a villager, for which he was confined, tried by a court-martial, and sentenced three hundred lashes. If I was disposed to connive at injuries done them, I would not prohibit, by beat of tom-toms, communication between the sepoys and inhabitants, or send to the head-man to inform the villagers to make me acquainted with any grievance they may receive from them.

No

I did myself the honour of delivering to your Excellency, for your perusal, my sentiments in a few rules that may be proper to be observed in the subordinate settlements. In two or three articles they exceed the intentions of the Court of Directors, in respect to the line that was drawn for the civil and military powers; but as they are calculated for the good of the service in general, and will tend to re-establish order and harmony, I flatter myself that they will be esteemed deserving of consideration.

I have the honour to be, &c.

Richard Mathews.

Madras, Feb. 21, 1778.

Rules

No cooleys were employed, to my knowledge, by any person, but by me, when I came here, for the benefit of my health, when each received a rupee, more I believe than is paid, for so short attendance, on similar occasions, in this district.

The necessaries for the use of the troops were mostly received from Ellore, in particular all the rice, and very little of any article was supplied by the village. The customs of the place were never interfered with, by me, or my authority, or were any received for my use but what were my right, such as resulted from the sale of articles in the buzar established for the use of the detachment; and them were regulated by a bramin now at Buzwara, at so moderate a rate, that a villager, who rented them at fifty rupees a month, would not continue it, as he said, on such dear terms.

As I hope I have sufficiently exculpated myself in your opinion, from the groundless charges of the Tanadar, beg leave to request you will be pleased to represent the same to the chief and council of Masulipatam, that, in case the Tanadar cannot prove his assertions, they will be pleased to have him punished as he deserves, for advancing such falsehoods.

I am, very respectfully, Sir,

Your very obedient, humble servant,

Ellore, Nov. 27, 1778.

James Rugg.

Rules, Orders and Regulations, for the better observance of the orders of the Hon. Company, respecting the several setttlements subordinate to Fort St. George, delivered to Sir Eyre Coote, by Major Mathews.

1. The commanding officer of the troops in the district to have a seat at the board, as second in council in that subordinacy, in all cases military, political and of revenue.

2. The political controul of the troops to be vested in the chief and council.

3. All general orders, respecting the motions of the troops, to be issued through the commanding officer in the district, excepting in cases of necessity, arising from the absence of the commanding officer at a place distant from the part threatened.

4. Military detail in the fullest sense to be vested in the commanding officer, who is to have power to appoint all officers to command garrisons, posts, cantonments, &c. The chief and council not to interfere with this branch of military arrangement.

5. Time of relief of troops to be determined by the commanding officer, with the concurrence of the chief and council.

6. Strength of all detachments for any service, with the quantity of stores, to be determined by the commanding officer of the troops in the district.

7. The chiefs of the subordinate factories of Masulipatam, Vizagapatam, Gangain, and Cuddalore, not to have any authority over the military in those garrisons, and are not in any respect to be considered as the governor of a garrison.

8. It being against the honourable company's orders that residents have the controul of military troops. They are in future not to have any, and to confine themselves to their civil department.

9. By

9. By the company's regulations in 1763, they direct that all officers, having a detached command, do attentively observe the conduct of the Polygars near them. The security of the company's possessions requires the most vigilant attention to what is doing on their frontiers, as well as by their secret enemies on their own lands, or by their armed or unarmed tributaries. Therefore, all officers in command are to observe with exact scrutiny what is doing near their posts, and to give the commanding officer constant and early advice of every occurrence, that evil may be timely prevented.

10. The commanding officer, where there are a chief and council, to have a certain number of Lascars put immediately under his orders, for the service of the artillery on the ramparts, or other garrison occasions.

11. Commanding officers of all detachments, posts, or garrisons are to afford every possible protection to the inhabitants, are not on any pretence to suffer them to be oppressed, nor their cattle seized, nor Coolies to be forced to labour without an adequate recompence.

12. Commanding officers of all separate detachments to contersign all bills of disbursements for their detachments, which are to serve as the paymaster's vouchers: and the commading officer of the troops in the district to countersign all the general and particular accounts of the paymaster before they can be deemed admissible by the chief and council.

Major Mathews, to Sir Eyre Coote, K. B. Lieutenant-General, &c.

Sir,

As I should be glad of taking the earliest, as well as the speediest opportunity of returning to Europe, I beg leave to put your Excellency in mind of the letter that I did myself the honour of addressing to you, under date the 16th instant, and shall be happy at

being

being permitted to go by the firſt ſhip that ſails. The ſucceſs galley is now under diſpatch for Suez, and I am informed that the Nabob conſents to my having a paſſage upon her.

I have the honour, &c.

Richard Mathews.

Madras, Feb. 22, 1779.

Colonel Owen, to Major Matthews.

Sir,

I am this minute directed by Lieutenant-General Sir Eyre Coote to acquaint you, that you may proceed to Europe, firſt reſigning your commiſſion in the honourable Company's ſervice, agreeable to the late orders of the Court of Directors in like caſes. Permit me to aſſure you that

I am, ſir, your moſt obedient ſervant,

Arthur Owen, Aid de Camp.

Fort St. George, Feb. 23, 1779.

Major Mathews, to the Hon. Thomas Rumbold Eſq; Governor, &c. and Select Committee.

Honourable Sir, and Sirs,

The month of October 1776 began the eighteenth year that I had ſerved the honourable company, as an officer, in almoſt every ſcene of actual ſervice that had occurred. In which time the beſt part of my life had been exerted in a ſhare of ſubduing the Carnatic, and extending the influence of our nation. In ſo long an abſence from my family many circumſtances muſt have happened that would induce a perſon of leſs feeling than myſelf to apply for leave to viſit once more thoſe connexions formed in infancy and youth, that are ever dear to a man the remainder of his days. An only daughter too demanded the care of the surviving parent to settle her in a place of security against the vices of the age. These were the motives that induced me to ask permission to go to England in October 1776. The detention of the ship Greenwich (on which I embarked) at different places lengthened our passage to nine months; so that I did not arrive in the British channel until the latter end of July 1777. Some time after my being in London, I heard that I had been superseded by the now Major Maclellan. Solliciting the Court of Directors for my lost rank took up much of my time; and I had every probability of succeeding, if assurances upon honour from gentlemen in public characters are to be depended upon; who were informed that I declined serving beneath my proper station on the list of the army on this establishment, or, without being removed with advantage to another. While the matter remained unconcluded, owing to the powerful influence of Major Maclellan's friends, I was employed in arranging my family concerns, and had not any thoughts of returning to India till every thing was so determined, that my mind being at peace, I should be enabled to exert effectually the experience gained under able officers of cavalry and infantry, of his Majesty's land forces, and those educated in the service of the company.

When I was at Chester, I received notice that the chairman, Mr. Wombwell wanted me on particular business. Upon my waiting on him, he requested that I would take dispatches, of the first importance, to India over land. This was a most difficult task, as I only know the language of an Englishman; but I did not suffer it to check my inclinations of doing good service to the state. Relying on the promise of the Court of Directors, I chearfully took the disagreeable journey, and was happy in performing it so as to answer the purpose of my mission. I will not conceal that the solemn promise of my rank being restored was a powerful motive to my accepting the office of a herald; but at the same time I declared,

that

that if my appointment was not sent by the first ship, I should return to England, to remove the bar in my way to those honours due to long and faithful services.

Since my arrival in India the records will, I hope, shew how I have been employed.

I have done myself the honour of addressing Sir Eyre Coote, under date the 3d of January, the 16th and 22d of February on the subject of my rank, and the treatment that I suffered whilst in the command of the troops in the district of Masulipatam, and applied for permission to return to England. The answer that I yesterday received, "That I might proceed to Europe, first resigning my "commission in the company's service," is couched in such slighting terms, that I would wish to think it a mistake, because there is not, any nation that have not been careful of preserving their old experienced officers whom they have reason to know are firmly attached to the service.

I therefore beg leave to inform your Honour, &c. that the short time I was in England was not sufficient to settle those concerns that were the object of my going there in 1776; and that they were left by my sudden departure disarranged: that I shall on all occasions consider myself as a servant to the English East-India Company; and that if my immediate return to England can only be obtained upon the hard and cruel terms of abandoning the service of the company, that I lost the commission in the deserts of Arabia by which I should now act.

Since my return to India I have not received either pay or perquisite. Batta cannot be considered as such, not being sufficient to defray extraordinary expences; and I humbly request that this, and my standing in the service, may be referred to the pleasure of the Court of Directors.

I have the honour, &c.

Richard Mathews.

Madras, Feb. 23, 1779.

Major Mathews, to Charles Oakley, Esq; Military Secretary.

Sir,

The time for dispatching the ship upon which I would wish to embark is so near, that I find myself under the necessity of requesting to know if the honourable select committee have directed that an answer be given to my letter of the 23d ult. If not, and that you can with propriety put the Hon. President in mind of it, I beg the favour of your doing so.

I am, sir, your most obedient humble servant,

Richard Mathews.

Madras, March 1, 1779.

Mr. Oakley, the Military Secretary, to Major Mathews.

Sir,

I am directed by the President, and select committee, to acknowledge the receipt of your letter of the 23d ult. and to acquaint you that you have their permission to go to England agreeably to your request; but as the Hon. Court of Directors have expressly ordered that every servant of the company, who shall return from India, on account of his private affairs, or on any other account, except the recovery of health, shall be considered as totally out of the service; the President and select committee have it not in their power to grant you their leave upon any other terms. They will, however, agreeably

ably to your requeſt, mention to the Court of Directors the circumſtances attending your departure from India.

I am, ſir, your moſt obedient ſervant,

Charles Oakley, Secretary.

Major Mathews, to the Hon. Thomas Rumbold, Eſq; Governor, &c. and Select Committee.

I beg leave to lay before you notes for money advanced by me for the honourable company's ſervice, at the time that I commanded the troops in the diſtrict of Maſulipatam, and for what was laid out by lieutenants Brown and Ruſſel, who commanded ſeparate detachments; the firſt employed againſt Rajannah-doorah, who had invaded the Shankarum country; the latter had a light armed party, at the paſs of Bezoara ready to move at the ſhorteſt notice.

Numbers 1 and 2 were preſented to the chief and council, to which they ſent the accompanying reply. Had they the leaſt room to ſuppoſe that I made a perquiſite of the charges for ſecret ſervice, they would have done well to have repreſented the abuſe to your Honours, that bounds might be fixed which the moſt favoured ſhould not overleap. But of themſelves I cannot conceive, that they had authority to "ſtrike off," in ſuch an indecent manner half the ſum required; and which ſum is only two-thirds of what I really expended, as will appear by my books and note, number 3. That I did not draw for more than fifteen pagodas the former months, was, becauſe I did lay out more. If your Honours will be pleaſed to examine the accounts of other commands you will find that my charges are conſiderably leſs than what is monthly paid to others whoſe truſt and ſituation does not demand ſo much attention. Number 2, is for money advanced as therein mentioned. The military paymaſter, as well as the chief and council made a miſtake in the perſon's person's name. The poor man, Chelacauney Venkiah,* was by oppression so much reduced, that he had not wherewith to purchase a meal. My letters to the chief and council of the 13th, 15th 16th, and 18th of last December will inform your Honours why he was made a prisoner. Wanting money to bear his expences to Masulipatam, he applied to me, and I let him have as much as he required, fifty Madras pagodas. The orders of the 22d of December prevented an application from me to him for the sum; therefore I sent the note to the chief and council, who thought proper to return it. Chelacauney Venkiah was then at Masulipatam. I am now under the necessity of requesting that your Honours will order it to be paid.

In

* Memorandum taken the 17th of December, 1778, in presence of Lieutenant Forbes and Mr. Pearce.

The morning that Chelacauney Venkiah was brought as a prisoner to Chicacolum, one Narsapah, belonging to Mr. ———, came to me, attended by two men, as Havaldars, and nine, as Peons or Sepoys; these nine had English firelocks, pouches and bayonets. The Gomastah Narsapah said, that his master had lent Venkiah 1500 Pagodas, which, by interest, had, in the space of nine months, increased to 2000 Pagodas, which sum he was sent with those sepoys to demand; that Venkiah had daily put him off on some pretence, and now that he was seized (the Gomastah) did not know where to get the usual Batta for himself and people. To which I told him, that I should not interfere; but that I supposed Venkiah, in his present circumstances, was not able to give him any money, having accepted of fifty Pagodas from me.

Chelacauney Venkiah told my servant, that he only received one thousand Pagodas of Mr. ———: but that with the premium for advancing the money and other charges, Mr. ——— had obtained from him a bond for one thousand, five hundred Pagodas, which was now increased, by high compound interest, and other charges made upon him by Mr. ———'s servant, to near two thousand five hundred pagodas in only nine months; which was the reason that he was going over the Kistna to endeavour to pay off this debt that was rendered more burthensome every day. To the Gomastah and Sepoys he was obliged to pay four Pagodas per day, as batta. Venkiah said, that his debts to other gentlemen, mentioning their names, were encreased by the same means.

In August 1778, I was directed to raise as many sepoys as I could; it then became my duty to send recruiting parties wherever it seemed possible to procure any; to those who engaged to bring good men I promised a recommendation, according to the number brought: to some I advanced money, to others the paymaster did; among the former is a valuable young man, by name Beeajerow, a Marattoe, who had hopes by his exertions to be a Subadar in the service. At different times, I advanced him eighty-five Madras pagodas, since which money has been given to him by my desire, that I have not an account of; he brought from Cicacole to Ellore 48 sepoys, and delivered them, according to orders, to captain James Powell, who was the commanding officer. At this time orders were issued for disbanding the new-raised battalions, and his party dismissed. He had advanced them subsistence from the time that he enlisted them, which amounted to the sum mentioned: he (himself) went to Masulipatam, and I sent him with his accounts and necessary vouchers the old sepoys, who were lent him for his assistance in recruiting, to the chief, Mr. Cotsford. But the chief and council did not order that I should be repaid, or him any recompence for his trouble. I have therefore to request, that something may be done for him adequate to his services, from September to January inclusive; being the time that he was employed for the honourable Company, without any personal or pecuniary advantage; and that the money, 85 Madras pagodas, advanced by me to him for the public service, may be repaid. The amount due to me is, Madras pagodas, two hundred and forty-two, and three rupees. To lieutenant Archibald Brown, Madras pagodas, ninety-five, and seventy-two fanams. To lieutenant James Russel, rupees sixty.

I have the honour, &c.

Richard Mathews.

Madras, March 5, 1779.

Major

Major Mathews, to the Hon. Thomas Rumbold, Esq; Governor, &c. and Select Committee.

Honourable Sir, and Sirs,

I take the liberty of transmitting to your Honours sundry papers,* as per list, which I request may be made a number in the packet sent by the Mountstuart, now under dispatch for England, for the consideration of the honourable the Court of Directors.

I have the honour, &c.

Richard Mathews.

Madras, March 13, 1779.

Mr. Oakley, to Major Mathews.

Sir,

I am directed by the honourable the President and select committee to acknowledge the receipt of your letter, dated this day, and to acquaint you, that as the packet for the Mountstuart will be closed to-night,† they cannot, in justice to the chief and council of Masulipatam, transmit by that ship the several papers you have inclosed, by way of justification of your conduct to the Court of Directors, in the course of your disputes with them, since it would appear a manifest partiality to transmit any thing that reflects on their measures in proceedings towards you, without giving them an opportunity of replying thereto.

I am, sir, your most obedient servant,

Charles Oakley, Secretary.

Fort St. George, March 13, 1779.

Major

---

* The papers were extracts of public letters to and from the chief and council, with copies of petitions that Major Mathews had sent to them, and copies of letters to General Munro, and to Sir Eyre Coote.

† The Mountstuart did not sail until the 27th of March.

Major Mathews, to the Hon. Thomas Rumbold, Esq; President, and Select Committee of Fort St. George.

Honourable Sir, and Sirs,

In your reply that you honoured me with, in answer to my second application to go to England, you were pleased to grant me leave, at the same time said, that you could not do so upon any other terms than what were ordered by the honourable the Court of Directors, and that you would lay my request of being considered absent upon leave before the Court of Directors.

I consider my case a particular one, far different from any that at the time of forming the order, the honourable Directors could suppose would occur.

I have not been taught that the weak form of delivering up a commission was ever esteemed necessary; those that you have been pleased to consider as out of the company's service, you have notified as such, without the useless ceremony of receiving back to the secretary's office a bit of parchment, which, of itself, is of no value. Public orders are required to give it authority, or deprive it of power.

In the dispatches that I had the honour of bringing from London, I have reason to believe, that the Directors made no mention of my returning to my station on the coast. They were told that I could not act beneath my proper rank; and that if my commission was not sent by the first conveyance, I should return to England; especially as the business which induced me to go to Europe in October 1776, was not settled.

Last year I came to India, at the particular request of the chairman; and, at that time, had every good reason to consider myself as a private person employed for a special purpose, and not as an officer

officer returning to his duty. My being on service in the district dependent on Masulipatam, was, in some measure, at my own option, expecting that I should have an opportunity of distinguishing myself; and I beg it may be remarked, that I have served without pay. I take the liberty of mentioning these circumstances to shew, that my case is different from those officers whose desire of going to Europe is new, and has arose since the promulgation of the restraining orders.

On supposition that your honours had given me permission to return to England, under the afore-cited restrictions, which also was left to the consideration of the Court of Directors, I waited upon the Governor yesterday forenoon, to pay him the usual compliments, upon leaving the settlement: it is probable that I should not have gone farther than Pondicherry; but as it is my wish to be as expeditious as possible in getting to England, I did intend going to Tranquebar, if at Pondicherry I had received any hopes of procuring a passage from thence upon a Danish ship now there.

But Mr. Rumbold put a stop to my journey, by saying, "Sir, I tell you, as governor of the garrison, that you have not leave to go;" meaning to Europe. Copy of the conversation, as near the words and sense as I can recollect, I do myself the honour of inclosing. I presume once more to request permission to return to England, upon any terms that your Honours deem consistent with your trust and my services. As to a commission, I have already informed you, it is lost: if it rests with me to say that I consider myself out of your service, I do so, and beg I may be allowed to proceed, by the first convenient opportunity, upon the Shrewsbury, now under dispatch, if it is your pleasure.

I have the honour to be, with all due respect,

Honourable Sir, and Sirs, your most obedient servant,

Richard Mathews.

Madras, March 22, 1779.

Conversation on Sunday, March 21, 1779, between Governor Thomas Rumbold, Esq; and Major Mathews.

Major. Your servant, sir; (no reply in words) I purpose setting out for Pondicherry, if you have no objections.

Gov. Pondicherry; (sharply) any further, sir?

Major. Yes, if I can procure a passage in a Danish ship for Europe, I intend to go to Tranqebar.

Gov. Ah,— you should have mentioned Tranquebar; Pondicherry and Tranquebar are not the same; but, sir, have you leave to go to Europe?

Major. By the reply to my letter I consider myself as disengaged, and at liberty to return to England.

Gov. I think that you have not leave:—the letter,—what does it say?

Major. It begins with granting me leave to go to England; but that it must be upon the terms ordered by the Court of Directors: in consequence, I supposed that the select committee might consider me as out of the service.

Gov. Sir, you have been long in the military, and are not unacquainted with forms; you must resign your commission.

Major. I never conceived that the form of resigning, by delivering up a commission, was in such a case necessary; that it was in the power of the select committee to strike my name out of the list.

Gov. Sir, (angrily) I tell you, as Governor of the garrison, that you have not leave to go.

Major. No, sir;—then what must I do?

Gov. You must write to the board.

Major. I shall write to-morrow, sir. Your servant, sir.

SECOND PART.

Major Mathews, to Anthony Sadleir, Esq; Chief and Council of Masulipatam.

Gentlemen,

The honourable the President and secret committee having appointed me to command the troops in the Masulipatam district, and directed that the greatest part be forthwith assembled for the defence of the company's districts; I request that you will be pleased to acquaint the several commanding officers in the district, that they are to obey my orders, agreeably to the honourable company's regulations, and the rules of service.

I have the honour, &c.

Masulipatam, Aug. 13, 1778.

Richard Mathews.

The Chief and Council of Masulipatam, to Major Matthews, commanding the troops in Masulipatam, &c. Circars.

Sir,

We have received your letter of this day's date. Your appointment to the command of the troops in the Circars of this dependency, shall be made known to the several commanding officers therein, who will be required to publish it in the form and manner usual upon such occasions.

With respect to what you inform us, concerning the directions you have received from the President and select committee, for assembling

sembling the troops of this district, we can only reply, by acquainting you with their instructions to us, so far as it regards the conduct we are to observe to you, *viz.* " That we are to attend particularly " to Major Mathews's recommendations, and to afford him all pos- " sible assistance to forward the services expected from him."

Whatever arrangements that you may hereafter recommend to us will certainly be received with all the attention we are recommended to shew to them, and every assistance granted you in our power to afford.

We are, sir, your most obedient servants,

Anth. Sadleir.
James Hodges.
Thomas Barnard.

Masulipatam, Aug. 13, 1778.

Major Mathews, to Anthony Sadleir, Esq; chief and council of Masulipatam.

Gentlemen,

I have received your letter of the 13th. The arrangement which I recommended, as necessary to take place, is inclosed; also a list of the stores to be removed from Samulcotah and Ellore; and an indent for sundries for the use of the troops in the field. Whatever part of the indent you can at this time furnish may be sent with captain Johnstone, whom you will be pleased to order to the part mentioned, and give in general the necessary directions for supplies that the service may not be injured by delays.

That timely notice may be given of the approach of the enemy by sea; I beg leave to recommend that alarm posts be established at proper places on the coast, particularly at point Devi; and that Peons be stationed at convenient distances from each other along the beach, at least, 30 miles north and south. Alarm posts may also

also be formed from hence towards Condapilly, and to the troops that may be in the field to give notice by the discharge of cannon if succour is required at Masulipatam.

I have the honour, &c.

Richard Mathews.

Masulipatam, Aug. 15, 1778.

ARRANGEMENT.

The fort of Samulcotah to be evacuated, part of the artillery, ammunition and stores, as per accompanying list, to be sent with captain Powell to Ellore, the remainder to Masulipatam.

A serjeant, a Jemadar, two Havaldars, two Naikes, and forty sepoys to be left at Injeram, for the security of the honourable company's investment: of these a guard may be sent to Samulcotah, to take care of the stores until they are conveyed away, when two sepoys will be sufficient to look after the barracks.

Captain Powell, with his battalion, exclusive of the abovementioned, to march to Ellore.

The three companies of captain Bridges's battalion, now in Masulipatam, to join captain Bridges at Condapilly.

Lieutenant Meek to remain at Yentapollam.

Captain Johnstone, with his battalion, excepting the recruits, to proceed as soon as possible to take post on the northern bank of the Kistna, equi-distant from Condapilly and Masulipatam.

The sepoys and artillery now at Ellore to prepare for the field. Draft bullocks to be provided for four six pounders and their tumbrils.

Soon after captain Powell's arrival at Ellore, and that every thing necessary is prepared for the field, the troops will move from thence to the southward.

The stores now at Ellore, that may not be wanted for camp, or at Condapilly, will be sent to Masulipatam.

Captain

Captain Bridges will at a convenient time march from Condapilly, leaving two companies, or a number as shall then be deemed a security for the fortress.

When all the troops are together, that can at this time be collected, they will not amount to twelve hundred effective men, which with four six pounders, will be the whole force for the present security of the Circars, exclusive of the garrisons and posts.

The recruits of captain Johnstone's battalion will be equal to almost a complete company.

Richard Mathews.

Masulipatam, Aug. 15, 1778.

The Chief and Council of Masulipatam, to Major Mathews.

Sir,

We have received your letter under date the 15th, with the accompanying papers, and the arrangement of the troops which you recommend as necessary to take place.

In most of the particulars we concur in opinion with you, and will issue the necessary orders, that these may be carried into execution as soon as possible.

There are some few, however, in which our opinion differs widely from your's. These we will proceed to mention, and after we have stated our idea of them, we must desire your reply thereto. We cannot approve of your present disposition for the three companies of captain Bridges's battalion, nor that for captain Johnstone's battalion. Whilst they remain a part of this garrison, with the other troops in it, they are sufficient to protect it against any apparent danger; but without them we judge that this place, until the force you are assembling can be got together, so as we can have recourse to it for assistance, must be in a manner defenceless: for, in captain Rowles's battalion, there are little more than 300 effective men.

On

On the other hand, encamped as you propose captain Johnstone's battalion on the banks of the Kistna, and these three companies gone to Condapilly, we do not see (there being no immediate prospect of Mr. Lally's* coming into the country) of what use they can be at the above places; so that in our judgment, by removing them immediately from this garison, they will be taken from a station where they are much wanted, (that is to say, until your force is assembled) to place them where they are scarcely wanted at all. We think, therefore, they should remain here until the Samulcotah and Ellore parties will be able to meet them at the place of general rendezvous.

Neither can we approve of the post you recommend for the station of the camp on the banks of the Kistna, equi-distant from Condapilly and Masulipatam. We think it ought to be within twelve miles of this latter place; as it appears to us of much greater importance that you should be at hand to give speedy assistance to Masulipatam, than that you should be ten or twelve cofs more advanced to give an enemy the meeting. Of their approach you may, we suppose, rely on being early enough apprised so as to be able to meet them on our own borders; but by your being so much farther removed from hence, the enemy may gain time enough to accomplish their point by sea. We have not come to any resolution in these particulars, which we have suggested to your consideration. We desire first to know your further sentiments thereon, to which we wish to shew every attention that can possibly be expected from us.

We are, &c.

Anth. Sadleir,
James Hodges,
Thomas Barnard.

Masulipatam, Aug. 16, 1778.

Major

* Consul Lacy to the ir reports to the select committee, previous to my arrival.

Major Mathews, to Anthony Sadleir, Esq; chief and council of Masulipatam.

Gentlemen,

I have received your letter of the 16th instant. It is in vain for me to say more on the subject of stationing troops, or of the service that the honourable the President and select committee expect from the troops in the Circar, than what I have repeatedly told Mr. Sadleir, who has, as also Mr. Barnard, seen my orders from Madras. My opinion is still the same, and I can only say, that as far as lays in my power I will fulfil the intentions of the honourable board; whose orders and the regulations of the honourable company, will be my guide; at the same time not omitting a due observance to your requisitions.

I have the honour, &c.

Richard Mathews.

Masulipatam, Aug. 17, 1778.

The Chief and Council of Masulipatam, to Major Mathews.

Sir,

We have received your letter under date the 17th instant. We cannot but express our surprise, that in reply to our last, you should refer us to conversations with our chief: it was our desire, in order to save time and unnecessary trouble, to have had your opinion in the manner it was given to Mr. Sadleir: but we are told by him that on his proposing a meeting, it was declined by you; and, for that reason we cannot but consider your declaration, as far as it relates to him, as the more extraordinary. He begs leave to observe to you, for himself, that all his conversations were, as he understood them, quite of a private kind, not official; and that, considering them at the time in this light, he did not commit them to his memory; nor can bring to his recollection any circumstances, as mentioned by you, which have not already been communicated by letter. We are sorry to conclude this subject by observing, that upon a view of what has passed, your treatment of us appears to have been not a little abrupt.

We shall give you our sentiments once more, on the subject of the arrangements proposed by you; with some alterations that have arisen from maturer reflection, and then acquaint you with what we have resolved. We wish to forward the service you are sent upon to the utmost of our power; we think what we have to offer will have a tendency thereto; and although our opinions have differed, and possibly will differ, we shall make it our study to give you all possible assistance.

The Honourable the President and select committee having commanded the troops in the Circars to be assembled, to form a camp, and intrusted you with this object of their orders, uncertain whether they be discretionary or not, we can only give our opinion thereon; as from our situation on the spot things may have occurred to our observations, which could not have struck them, for want of a nearer view of them.

The country is in a perfect state of tranquility,* and from the situation of Basalat Jung, and the Soubah, the first of them, having a formidable enemy, Hyder Ally, hovering over his country, and the other equally threatened by the same enemy, no prospect of this peace being disturbed, we have nothing then, as we judge at present, to apprehend from the party under Mr. Lally; for Basalat Jung is in too alarming a situation to be able to part with so considerable a force as that under the command of Mr. Lally; and the latter, however

---

* Not true. The northern part had been alarmed some time; the southern also by Lally and his party, in the Guntoor Circar; and the western by the Soubah's preparations.

ever inclined, must be unable, for want of resources, to move from Adoni, without his master's concurrence; on whom alone he must, we apprehend, depend for such resources.

If the above statement of matters be a just one, we have scarcely any danger to apprehend but from the sea, our opinion is, that the *garrison of Samulcotah be withdrawn; the stores removed from Ellore to either Condapilly or Masulipatam, whichever may be thought proper.

The three companies of captain Bridges's battalion, now at Masulipatam, to march to Condapilly to join their corps.

The troops remaining at Masulipatam will then consist of captain Johnstone's and captain Rowles's battalions.

The troops of this Circar will thus be stationed at nearly an equal distance from the most convenient place of general rendezvous, on the banks of the Kistna, *viz.* at Condapilly, Ellore and Masulipatam, and may all march thither from their respective stations in one day, if they should be pressed for time.

They are all to be lightly equipped for service, and prepared to move at a moment's warning.

Although we are thoroughly persuaded there is no reason to apprehend Mr. Lally will be the first to move against us, a vigilant eye ought to be kept upon all his movements.

From the foregoing arrangements the following good effects will arise: Masulipatam will be protected: the additional expence of batta and field charges, so long as the troops continue inactive, be saved; and time given for disciplining and getting the new-raised sepoys into proper order.

---

* This shews that they either were, or for some design wished to appear ignorant of the invasion by Rajanah Dourah.

We are of opinion, which ought however to have been mentioned before, you have not sufficiently provided for the safety of Injeram, as we judge an officer requisite for the protection of the honourable company's property at that place.

The communication of our sentiments, as just explained to you, we consider a duty imposed upon us by our station, and we now proceed to acquaint you, that resolved to fulfil in the utmost extent what the honourable select committee have intimated to us, we shall immediately issue orders that your arrangements may take place, exactly as they are stated in the paper you gave in, charging you, however, with the responsibility for any events that may result therefrom, both as to the safety of this place, and the places dependent thereon.

We mean, in order to our justification for thus throwing on you the responsibility of the measures you have proposed to us, to lay before the honourable select committee our proceedings and correspondence on the occasion, which we would not do without previously intimating such our intentions.

We inclose you a requisition to captain Johnstone, that his battalion, and the three companies of captain Bridges's battalion, move to a place of encampment out of this fort; and we send this requisition to you, that you may name a spot for them to march to; after which both parties will pursue such orders as you have to give them, and of this they are informed.

We are, &c.

Anth. Sadleir,
James Hodges,
Thomas Barnard.

Masulipatam, Aug. 18, 1778.

Major Mathews, to Anthony Sadleir, Esq; chief and council of Mafulipatam.

Gentlemen,

*The following intelligence I received this morning from Ongole.

"That Bafalat Jung has fent orders to the †Rajah Bahauder to have pots, ſtraw, and wood, ready at different villages in the Circar in the road to Guntoor, for four thouſand ſepoys, and Lally's corps of Europeans. And further orders for Rajah Bahadar, to raiſe three thouſand recruits."

I muſt requeſt your affiſtance, that no more time be loſt in affembling the troops of this Circar, agreeably to the orders that I brought from the honourable the Preſident and ſecret committee.

All the ſtraggling ſepoys in this diſtrict that are with renters, or their managers, &c. &c. muſt forthwith join their battalions. And I beg that if you want any of the troops of this diſtrict for the ſervice of the honourable company, that you would do me the honour to conſider me in the ſame light, as the honourable company orders, by their regulations, that the commanding officer of the troops in the diſtrict ſhould appear; to whom requiſitions are to be made by the chief and council, if military affiſtance be wanting. In time of war it is neceſſary that this rule be ſtrictly obſerved; for I cannot be accountable for poſts, if their ſtrength be diminiſhed, or, probably entirely removed without my knowledge. It is alſo certain that the commander of a poſt ſhould know whom he is to obey. Theſe are points that will not admit of diſpute, and which, I hope, will not occaſion any; for I am determined to obſerve ſuch a line of conduct as ſhall merit the approbation of my ſuperiors.

If

---

* This letter was ſent to Mafulipatam about two hours before the receipt of the laſt of the ſame date.

† The perſon appointed by Bafalat Jung to have charge of the Guntoor Circar.

If I was at a great distance from Masulipatam it might, probably, be attended with small inconvenience the making at all times requisitions to me; in which case, orders should be issued to prevent an injury to the service. But at the very time that I am on the spot, your sending orders to captain Bridges, who commands the garrison nearest to the enemy, to detach sepoys to relieve some of captain Johnstone's, who are ordered to Masulipatam, is an indication that you wish to act against the spirit of public regulations, the rules of service, and the orders that I brought from Madras.

I have the honour to be, &c.

Richard Mathews.

Masulipatam, Aug. 18, 1778.

The Chief and Council of Masulipatam, to Major Mathews.

Sir,

We have received your letter of yesterday morning; we shall inclose a copy thereof to the honourable the President and select committee, and submit it to them to determine on the merits of it.

With respect to the detachments out on the service of the revenue in different parts of these districts, we can give you no positive reply; it has always been our endeavour to station none that are unnecessary: as soon as the business those that at present out are employed on, can be performed, they shall be required to join their respective corps.

With respect to the mode of procuring *sepoys guards for the service of the revenue, it may be necessary to observe to you, it is ordered by regulations on our records, that they shall be required from

---

* Their orders were direct interference with military detail. It was to relieve guards, and not a requisition for sepoys for revenue business.

from the officer commanding the garrisons nearest the place where they are to be on service. If it be your desire these requisitions should pass from you to these officers, we have no objections; but there must be an exception in all cases where the service would be materially injured by the delay of sending these requisitions to you.

We are, &c.

Anth. Sadleir,
James Hodges,
Thomas Barnard.

Masulipatam, Aug. 19, 1778.

Major Mathews, to Anthony Sadleir, Esq; chief and council of Masulipatam.

Gentlemen,

As you are sorry to be forced to observe my being abrupt, I am truly so at being under the necessity of endangering an increase of your displeasure.

Your seeming determination to pursue sentiments contrary to the express orders of the honourable the President and secret committee, and to my opinion, of which you were verbally made acquainted the morning after my arrival; which opinion was founded upon the nature of the service that the honourable board expected from the troops of this Circar; and notwithstanding several conversations with Mr. Sadleir on the subject, the last continuing above an hour, and was on the morning of the day of your meeting that he desired me to attend the board. I could not help thinking that it would not answer any good purpose to be interrogated by those whom (as I suppose) had already formed their plan. I told the chief that I did not chuse to attend; because he knew my sentiments upon every point, and my particular orders from Madras, all of which he might com-

communicate to the council that was immediately to affemble; and furely he could not in a few minutes forget what I underftood was the the very bvfinefs of his morning vifit. You will, I hope, no longer think it extraordinary that I fhould decline needlefs repetitions; and be convinced that Mr. Sadleir's converfation with me was official, when I tell you, that he promifed to inform the council therewith.

If words have force, you will underftand what is meant by the following extract of my orders from Madras.

" We defire you particularly to watch the motions of Mr. Lally, who has a confiderable force in the Guntoor Circar, and to act with the troops under your command in the beft manner poffible for the defence of the company's diftricts; or occafionally on the offenfive againft the French troops with Mr. Lally, as the circumftances of affairs may render moft eligible."

To act according to the fpirit of thefe orders, the troops fhould be in the field. You were informed that fuch was the intention of the honourable the Prefident and fecret committee; they alfo told you, that a battalion was to compofe the garrifon of Mafulipatam, which battalion only confifted of eight companies, and could not be more than five hundred effective men. Upon my arrival captain Johnftone's battalion amounted to four hundred, fixty-feven; whofe battalion might have remained in garrifon, had not you ordered captain Rowles's in without my knowledge. Captain Rowles has now near four hundred men fit for duty; with thefe there will be left a company chiefly compofed of captain Johnftone's recruits, two-thirds of them expert in the ufe of their arms, and fit to join the battalion: fo that the garrifon will confift of near five hundred effectives, two hundred (as I am told) good Lafcars, ten European artillery, and twenty European infantry; alfo the invalids that were lately ordered to Madras, who are now on their return to Mafulipatam; the

fick

sick of captain Rowles's battalion will be daily recovering and the absentees joining; all these form a force full sufficient to guard against a sudden attack.

The troops in the field will make the safety of Masulipatam the principal object of their attention; at the same time they will not be blind to the dangers that may ensue from such a force as Lally's, and the present uncertain (as far as we know of the) intentions of Basalat Jung, the Soubah, or Hyder.

I have sent the orders to captain Johnstone, and shall chearfully accept of the responsibility for any measures that can be taken for the defence of the company's districts with such a small force as is in this Circar.

With the correspondence that in your letter of the 18th, you say, you intend to send to the honourable select committee, let me request that you would be pleased to send a copy of this.

I have the honour to be, &c.

Richard Mathews.

Masulipatam, Aug. 19, 1778.

Mr. Barnard, to Major Mathews.

Sir,

I am commanded by the chief and council to send the inclosed extract of a letter they are now dispatching to the honourable the President and select committee; and further to acquaint you, that they do not mean to send any other reply to your letter to them under date the 19th instant.

I have the honour to be, sir,

Your most obedient servant,

Thomas Barnard.

Masulipatam, Aug. 20, 1778.

Major Mathews, to Anthony Sadleir, Esq; chief and council of Masulipatam.

Gentlemen,

I have been favoured with your letter of the 19th. I do myself the honour of informing you, that to-morrow I set out for Cicacole, and from thence mean to go to Condapilly, to put that fortress in a state of defence. I shall also take this opportunity of gaining a knowledge of the country between this place and Condapilly, which may be considered as part of our frontiers towards the enemy.

I shall at all times be ready to receive your commands, and have the honour to be,

Gentlemen, &c.

Richard Mathews.

Masulipatam, Aug. 20, 1778.

The Chief and Council of Masulipatam, to Major Mathews.

Sir,

We have received your letter of the 20th instant. We have been informed by the storekeeper at Ellore, that he had been applied to to furnish certain stores to be sent by your orders to Condapilly. Although we directed him to comply therewith, that no delay might happen to the service, we must beg leave to inform you, that such a procedure is irregular; and that stores are not to be conveyed to or from any of the garrisons, without an order from this board: you will please, therefore, in future, to make your application to us.

We send you inclosed a copy of a letter we have received from captain Powell. (*see p.* 99.) As to the protection of the country, is a trust with which you have charged yourself, and all responsibility of that kind rests with you, we refer the consideration of the matter

con-

contained in the above letter of captain Powell to you, desiring you will provide in the most effectual manner for the safety of those places which are now under such alarm.

We have also directed captain Powell to consult you with respect to the prisoners he mentions, and he will pursue such orders as you may please to give him regarding them.

The measure you have lately adopted of withdrawing the sepoy detachments on revenue service,* belonging to the garrison of Ellore, from their stations, of which we have been informed by lieutenant Moslay, will be attended with consequences highly prejudicial to the country and revenue. You will do well, therefore, carefully to weigh this matter; for determined as we are not to give the least obstruction to your measures, you must be accountable for all their effects. We shall no otherwise interfere, than by cautions of the above kind, where we judge you may not be aware of the consequences of your plan of operations.

We have no intelligence whatever to communicate from the country.

We are, &c.

Anthony Sadleir,
James Hodges,
Thomas Barnard.

Masulipatam, Aug 24, 1778.

Mr. Powell, to Anthony Sadleir, Esq; chief and council of Masulipatam.

Gentlemen,

Accompanying this I send you a return of recruits entertained for my battalion, agreeable to the General Orders of the 6th of July for augmenting the companies.

I beg

* Employed on the business of the paymaster's Dubash.

I beg leave to put you in mind of the prisoners in confinement here, (in number five, four men and a woman; one of the men the father of Rajanah-dourah, formerly the Rajah of Tottapillee) and requeſt you will inform me what is to be done with them.

The inhabitants of Paddapore, Pettapore and Samulcotah are already moving their effects to Jaggenautporam, and they inform me, that they themſelves will follow as ſoon as I march, in conſequence of a report that Rajanah-dourah is raiſing troops with an intent of coming hither to releaſe his father.*

I am, &c.

James Powell.

A true Copy. *Thomas Barnard,* Secretary.

Samulcotah, *Aug.* 22, 1778.

The Chief and Council of Maſulipatam, to Major Matthews

Sir,

We have received ſome orders from the honourable the Preſident and the ſelect committee,† which, agreeably to the rule we have laid down for our preſent conduct, until an anſwer comes to our reference on theſe matters, we ſhall communicate to you; that on our part no ſtep may be hazarded, that can poſſibly interfere with your arrangements. You will conſider us as no more than the channel by which theſe orders come to you from the honourable ſelect committtee, the moment you receive them from us, our concern in them

---

* Rajanah-dourah commenced his operations the 20th of July 1778, and entered the Tontapilly country the beginning Auguſt; it, therefore, ſeems extraordinary that captain Powell ſhould not have acquainted the chief and council of the invaſion, or, that they ſhould be ignorant of it until captain Powell was removed from his command at Samulcotah, to march towards the Kiſtna.

† Theſe orders from the ſelect committee inconſiſtent with their orders to Major Mathews.

them ceases, and you become answerable for the effects thereof. The honourable select committee have been pleased to direct, that we station a company of sepoys, with a prudent officer, at Yanam, to take charge of the property, that has been seized there. And further, that they having come to a resolution of seizing such Frenchmen as may be at Neirpollee, near to Vantipollam, do direct us to give the proper instructions to lieutenant Meck for that purpose.

We shall offer you our opinion as to this latter particular, as to what we think will be proper instructions for lieutenant Meck; and this is, that such of these Frenchmen as are in the character of gentlemen, be admitted on their parole, and sent in that manner to Ongole or Yanam, the choice of either places to be left to them; and all others to be sent prisoners to Ongole, taking care on no account to touch any private property.

We are, &c.

Anth. Sadleir,
James Hodges,
Thomas Barnard.

Masulipatam, Aug. 26, 1778.

Mr. Barnard, to Major Mathews.

Sir,

I am directed by the chief and council to inform you, that this moment received the accompanying letter, with another, addressed them from the honourable the President and select committee.

The honourable select committee therein acquaint them, that four French ships had left Pondicherry road, and had been seen the 22d instant off Sadrass: that they thought it probable them ships might endeavour to make a diversion somewhere on the coast; and that this intelligence was communicated, that the chief and council might be prepared against the danger.

The

*The honourable select committee further add, that they had directed you to take such measures for the defence of this place, and the port of Coringy, as might appear to you necessary.

I have been commanded by the chief and council to communicate the particulars to you.

I have the honour, &c.

Masulipatam, Aug. 27, 1778.

Thomas Barnard, Secretary.

Major Mathews, to Anthony Sadleir, Esq; chief and council of Masulipatam.

Gentlemen,

Since I addressed you the 20th of August, I have been at Condapilly. The fortifications are in a bad condition, and only two gun-carriages capable of bearing the discharge of a gun, without falling to pieces; it is necessary that a number be immediately sent there, of which a list is inclosed.

The magazine being already well stored, and from its situation insecure, except there was a very large garrison, I have ordered to Masulipatam all the ammunition and stores that were intended to be sent from Ellore, to Condapilly.

Having received from lieutenant Meek information that a Frenchman, at the head of four or five hundred sepoys, with some small guns, was within ten cofs of him; that Mr. Lally had applied to Basalat Jung, for leave to assist the French; that orders had been sent by Basalat Jung to different places on the road from Adoni towards Guntoor, to provide pots, wood, &c. for a large body of troops; and likewise that Mr. Hornet in the Guntoor Circar was raising sepoys, giving from five to seven rupees, per man, advance-money.

On

" See how consistent this with the select committee's orders to the chief and council. See the last letter.

On confideration of the above, I have ordered captain Bridges with a hundred men from Condapilly, who, with three companies now under lieutenant Doveton, a hundred men from Ongole, and lieutenant Meek's company, will form a detachment to fecure that part of the Circar fouth of the Kiftna, and to act as occafion requires, fhould any part of our country be threatened from the Guntoor Circar, or from the fea.

Lieutenant Doveton is by this time at Sandole, alfo the Ongole fepoys, waiting for captain Bridges.

Lieutenant Meek, upon the approach of the French party beforementioned, was ordered to retire to Sandole; thefe feparate parties, upon being joined by captain Bridges, will again advance to the fouthward.

Of the boats, that were at Cicacole, I have removed three to Sawlempollam, and two to Nauggalanka, that the communication to captain Bridges may be fpeedier and more convenient to the troops at Gundoor, and nearer to Mafulipatam. Thefe boats, after the paffage of the Tumbrills for Madras, may be reduced to one at each place; but this matter cannot be determined at this time.

I have received your letters of the 25th and 26th inftant. Capt. Powell is directed to provide for the alarmed inhabitants, and to fend the prifoners here.

A company is ordered to Yanam; and lieutenant Meek is directed to fecure the Frenchmen.

I have been honoured with a letter from the Prefident and felect committee, dated the 22d inftant, and one from Mr. Secretary Barnard, of this day's date. As much care as poffible fhall be taken for the general fecurity of the honourable company's Circars, by

Gentlemen, &c.

Richard Mathews.

Camp at Gundoor, Aug. 27, 1778.

Major

Major Mathews, to Anthony Sadleir, Esq; chief and council of Masulipatam.

Gentlemen,

The store-room at Condapilly, which is situated on that part of the rock that is defensible for a small garrison, is in need of repair; there are also some buidings that require immediate repair, and it is necessary to erect others on the hill for the conveniency of the troops. I should be glad that you would be pleased to order workmen, and materials for the above, which may be soon done and at little expence. The commanding officer at Condapilly will shew the workmen what they are to do.

I have the honour, &c.

Richard Mathews.

Camp, Aug. 29, 1778.

The Chief and Council of Masulipatam, to Major Mathews.

Sir,

We have received your letters of the 27th and 29th instant. The work you recommend at Condapilly cannot be put in hand until you favour us with an estimate of the expence. As soon as that is received, if the cost appears so trifling as to make a reference to the Presidency unnecessary, an order will be sent to begin it immediately.

Our chief having received a letter from the manager of Basili Jung, in the Guntoor Circar, the contents of which we think it necessary to communicate to you, a copy thereof accompanies this letter, with its answer.

We are, &c.

Anth. Sadleir,
James Hodges,
Thomas Barnard.

Masulipatam, Aug. 30, 1778.

Major

Major Mathews, to Anthony Sadleir, Esq; chief and council of Mafulipatam.

Gentlemen,

I have been favoured with your's of the 30th inſtant, incloſing copies of letters from and to Bafalat Jung's manager.

I am unacquainted with the expence of building; but imagine that every thing which is neceſſary to be done at Condapilly will not exceed five hundred rupees.

I have the honour, &c.

Richard Mathews.

Aug. 31, 1778.

Tranſlation of a letter from Rajah Beerjevendoſs, manager of Guntoor Circar, to the chief of Mazulipatam, dated the 3d Shaben moon, or 26th of Auguſt, and received the 28th of Auguſt, 1778.

For the friendſhip and good underſtanding which has always ſubſiſted between my maſter and the company, as well as the ſtrong friendſhip between you and me, we found that the company have the like deſire, by finding no difference between their country and my maſter's.

You have wrote me, ſome time ago, that your troops have occaſion to go to the ſouthward, and on their way to accommodate them with every thing neceſſary on ſuch occaſions, and that you have cautioned the officers commanding them not to ſuffer them, on any account, to diſturb my maſter's country, which made me very happy. But, at preſent, it is ſaid, that the company have revoked their opinions, all to the contrary we expected from them, regarding theſe Circars. I cannot give credit to theſe reports; however, to give you the proof of my friendſhip, I thought proper to acquaint you of;

P if

if sometime such is your opinion, I could have wished it had been explained in a clearer manner, that we may alter it accordingly.

Both I and my master never intend doing the least thing that will interrupt our friendship, therefore we shall do nothing that will cause your displeasure; trusting to your friendship and assistance, we have kept no large body of troops all this while in the country, but some time my master used to send out a few of his troops to frighten the Zemindars of these Circars.

There is no difference, upon any account, between us; for my own part, I think both the company's and my master's country are equal. Write me particularly of your intentions, I shall thereupon clear you up the doubt.

If I do not make my best endeavours to suppress your suspicions, you may think I act with you unfriendly.

I beg an answer to this as soon as possible.

The Answer.

To Rajah Beerjevendoss, Amuldar of Guntoor.

Aug. 30.

I have received your letter, dated the 26th of this month. The assurances you give me, as well in your master's name as in your own, of your intentions and wish to preserve amity and friendship with the company, are pleasing and satisfactory to me. I hope nothing will ever happen to interrupt the present good understanding between the company and Bazalat Jung.

When I wrote to you of some of our troops being going to the southward, and along the border of the Guntoor country, it was with intention to remove any apprehensions such movement might have occasioned you. Your orders for supplying them with provisions and coolies, I consider a proof of your master's friendly disposition

sition to the company, and have represented your behaviour to my superiors accordingly.

By advice received some time since from Europe, we have reason to believe a war will soon ensue between our nation and that of France; hostilities had commenced in Europe, by the detention of the English vessels in the ports of France.

Our government have determined to adopt the same mode of conduct against France in this country, and have already possessed themselves of the French settlements in Bengal, and on this coast, except Pondicherry, which place our army and fleet have now invested. The French ships left Pondicherry road, on seeing ours, who, in an action, a short time ago, defeated them. I hope I shall soon be empowered to inform you that Pondicherry is in our possession.

The troops stationed at present on the borders of your country, is not with intention to disturb the peace of it. Understanding that your master Bazalat Jung, has, for some years past, engaged a French party in his service, commanded by Mr. Lally, and that he is in great trust and confidence with your master, commanding, as I am informed, the whole of his forces; and not knowing, in these times, what conduct he may pursue, my suspicions have thought proper to have a watchful eye on this man's motions, as well as the party he is said to command. Nevertheless, we have always considered this force the force of Bazalat Jung, acting under his order, and subject to his authority. To this time I have no cause to think otherwise; and, to preserve the friendship which has long subsisted, and to remove all suspicions of your master's interference in the war between us and France, I shall hope your master will not consent to Mr. Lally's forces coming into the Guntoor Circar at this time. Assurances that he will not, I shall be very happy to receive from you, and such conduct will, no doubt, insure continuance of friendship with the company.

Our intentions of war are against the subjects of France only: we have no thought of disturbing the peace of the inhabitants of the Guntoor Circar; but hearing that a few Frenchmen are near the sea coast, at a village called Nairpillee, to prevent inconveniency from them, and to remove all possible cause of distrust your master, my superiors have thought proper to order such Frenchmen as are now there, or that may hereafter come by sea there, to be seized and made prisoners. And I trust you and your master will believe such action as intended for no other view than to promote the friendship between you and the company, by removing such cause of distrust.*

Major Mathews, to Anthony Sadleir, Esq; chief and council of Masulipatam.

Gentlemen,

In consequence of my directions, captain James Powell brought with him the prisoner Yankanah-dourah, the father of Rajanah-dourah, whom it was reported raised such an alarm at Peddapore, Pettapore, and the village of Samulcotah. The person that threatened those parts, it seems, wanted to obtain his †father's liberty. Some days ago I wrote to Rajanah-dourah to dismiss his new-raised levies, and wait the justice of the expected chief, Mr. Cotsford, who, I made no doubt, would release his father.

I am told that Yencanah-dourah has been confined near twelve months; is very old, and, if enlarged, could not be of any disservice; or, as a prisoner, of any service to the company; whereas, if he had his liberty, it might induce his son to be quiet, and leave his claims on the Tontapilly country to be decided by the honourable select

---

* On the 27th of August, (see my letter of that date) the chief and council were informed of the preparations for Lally's advance, of Mr. Hornet's raising sepoys, of Hornet's party, and that captain Bridges was then going over the river, and would have 500 men with him.

† See letter from captain Powell to the chief and council, dated Aug. 22.

select committee, which, at this time, would be a great point gained, by enabling me to draw to the Kistna that force which must otherwise be kept for the security of Peddapore, &c. I have, therefore, released Yencanah-dourah; and he has promised to use his influence with his son to prevent any disturbance.

    I have the honour to be, &c.

              Richard Mathews.

Camp at Gundoor, Sept. 4, 1778.

Major Mathews, to Anthony Sadleir, Esq; chief and council of Masulipatam.

Gentlemen,

I do myself the honour of informing you, that, for the conveniency of forage, I have moved the camp to Guntasaulla; and that, having received intelligence of the arrival of Mr. Lally, with a hundred horse at Innacondah, I have sent a detachment of sepoys and artillery over the Kistna.

    I have the honour to be, &c.

              Richard Mathews.

Camp, Sept. 8, 1778.

Major Mathews, to Anthony Sadleir, Esq; chief and council of Masulipatam.

Gentlemen,

The only intelligence that I have received from Adoni, by my own people is, that on the 29th ult. Mr. Lally was near Adoni. There was not making any extraordinary preparations for his marching; but he was encamped, and had every thing necessary for his moving. It was reported that after the Desarey feast he would certainly

tainly come this way with his own troops and Basalat Jung's cavalry.

Mr. Hornet and Rajah Bahauder, with two three pounders, one six pounder, five hundred sepoys, some Europeans, and a number of Peons, are at Potteram, ten or twelve cofs from the Baumpettah, and that their advanced guard was within three cofs of captain Bridges.

I have ordered over the Kistna captain Powell's battalion and two three pounders. Should there not assemble a greater force, in the Guntoor Circar, than what we already know of, captain Bridges, with the detachment of his battalion, will in a few days re-crofs the Kistna, and may go to Condapilly.

Captain Powell will have directions to cantoon his detachment in some convenient village, to secure them against the approaching rains.

I should be glad to know if you approve of the village of Gundoor, as a cantonment for captain Johnstone's battalion during the rains; if not, that you will pleased to point out a better situation.

I hear that Rajanah-dourah is besieging Routtapundah, a fort in the Tontapilly country, garrisoned by Timrauze. At this unhealthy season, I think it would be imprudent to send any of our troops among the hills that hath already been so fatal to our countrymen. I would with to defer bringing Rajanah-dourah to reason till the healthy time; and for the present secure as much as possible the Peddapore, and other districts, near Samulcotah, which I fancy may be done by a small detachment.

I have this moment heard from Condapilly, that one thousand black horse, and three battalions of sepoys have come to Combamet.

If this proves true, we must not think of the afore-mentioned cantoonments.

I have the honour to be, &c.

Richard Mathews.

Camp, Sept. 11, 1778.

P. S. Since writing the above I have received a letter from the select committee, dated Sept. 6, 1778, and shall observe their orders.

Major Mathews, to Anthony Sadleir, Esq; Chief and Council of Masulipatam.

Gentlemen,

I send you an extract of a letter that I have received from the honourable select committee, dated Sept. 6, 1778.

" As we do not find by the latest intelligence we have received, that Mr. Lally is moving from Adoni, we are of opinion, that it is unnecessary to make any detachments from your force at present, as it may give much alarm to the inhabitants, and hinder the collection of the revenues. We desire, therefore, that you will fix your camp in some proper situation for the security of the district; and not move any troops towards the Guntoor Circar, without further orders, or without the concurrence of the chief and council of Masulipatam."

I have, in consequence of the foregoing, sent orders to captain James Powell to re-cross the Kistna with all the troops of this district that are now to the southward of the river.

I have the honour, &c.

Richard Mathews.

Camp, Sept. 12, 1778.

The Chief and Council of Masulipatam, to Major Mathews.

Sir,

We have received your letters under date the 8th and 11th inst.

We address you now in consequence of a dispatch we yesterday received from the honourable select committee. They have therein communicated to us their sentiments on the subject of those differences in opinion, which have lately subsisted between us; and in doing this they have been pleased to express a very anxious desire of seeing harmony re-established in all measures which may affect the public service.

We should therefore esteem ourselves exceedingly deficient in what we owe to our trust, and highly wanting in that submissive deference we wish at all times to manifest to the opinions of our superiors, if we did not, to the utmost of our power, contribute to so desirable an end. With a view to this, we embrace with pleasure such an occasion of renewing the assurances of our sincere desire to co-operate with, and aid you in all particulars where our interference can be of service. Determined, on our part, studiously to avoid every ground of disagreement, we flatter ourselves, that if cases should unexpectedly start up, where some little difference of opinion is absolutely inevitable, that these dispositions in us, being aided and strengthened by similar ones on your part, any ill effects which might have happened otherwise, from such difference of opinion, will easily be prevented by the effect of our joint wishes to preserve unanimity, and by our mutual zeal for the good of the service. We shall here drop this subject, and proceed to the mention of certain particulars, on which we have received the orders of the honourable the president and select committee, in their above letter.

The

The utmost care has always been taken by us, not to employ sepoys on revenue services, unnecessarily. We removed many, previous to your arrival, and had it at the same time under deliberation to withdraw them all, but the necessity of the service would not allow of it; we are sorry to inform you that this necessity still exists, and obliges us to require that all the sepoys ordered from their stations on revenue service be remanded to them.

We now proceed to the consideration of what is contained in your letter of the 11th inst. Preparatory thereto, we think it necessary to acquaint you with the intelligence received by our chief, concerning the views and operations of the country powers in these parts. It may not be unnecessary to premise, that this is intelligence, which, in point of authority, is the best, we judge, that can be had, the persons who furnish it having approved themselves, by long service, men of discretion and fidelity. Our chief has received an answer from the manager of the Guntoor Circar, which removes all apprehension of immediate disturbances to any of our possessions in that neighbourhood. Mr. Lally is still at Adoni, and we hope will not advance from thence toward Guntoor. The manager has transmitted to his master our chief's letter, and has assured us that the *troops now in his country are merely for the purpose of collection. We are of opinion, therefore, that all the troops may repass the river, leaving only Lieutenant Meek at Vantapollam, as before. We do not mean, however, to lay your conduct under any restraint in this particular; we offer it as opinion only. With respect to what you men-

---

* The French had at this time a considerable party in the Guntoor Circar, under Monsieur Arno, who was employed in collecting the revenues of certain districts for the sole support of the French party under Monsieur Lally, and to receive military stores and recruits, landed at a sea-port belonging to Bazalat Jung, called Neerpilly, situated about thirty miles north of Ongola, adjoining to our Circar called Nizampatnam.

mention concerning the troops assembling in the Combamet Circars, the intelligence is, in part, only true, the force assembled not amounting to the numbers you informed us of, and we do not apprehend any present danger from that quarter. The Naib of that country, Fauzel beg Cawn, has always been considered as a friend to the company; and a †person of trust is, at his own desire, on the point of departure for Heiderabad, to confer with him. As soon as they meet, we shall be informed, with some degree of certainty, for what purpose these troops have been sent into that country. Until then, considering this country as under the management of one in the interest of our employers, that the force assembled is inconsiderable, we think it will be sufficient for any present appearance, to order captain Bridges's battalion to Condapilly, as you propose, and to keep a strict look out that way.

The cantooning of the troops will, in our opinion, be attended with unnecessary expence, as they may be put into good quarters, where they will find every accommodation, so necessary in bad weather, in a situation where they will be as near at hand to protect the country as in any place that could be chosen for a cantonment. We mean, by sending captain Powell's battalion to Ellore, and captain Johnstone's battalion to this place, besides the saving, in point of expence, the country will be benefited, as the alarm occasioned by the late movements will have time to subside.

We agree in opinion with you, that it would be imprudent to undertake any operations of importance against Rajanah Doorah, until the sickly season in the Totapilly districts is past, as we cannot be too attentive to keep the troops in health and spirits; we think therefore it would be adviseable to station captain Lane's battalion, now on their march this way, at Samulcotah, as we judge from the state

it

---

† A Dubash. See letter of the 13th December.

it is said to be in, that the whole strength of it will be no more than * sufficient for that service; perhaps it may be able to afford a relief for all the parties of captain Powell's battalion, now in that country, which, in that case, we think, should be ordered to join their corps; but of this we leave you the judge.

We would recommend that Lieutenant Brown should be stationed at Samulcotah, be ordered still to keep himself in readiness for marching, and without loss of time.

We are, &c.

Anth. Sadleir.
James Hodges.
Thomas Barnard.

This letter had no date, but was received by Major Mathews, Sept. 13, 1778.

Major Mathews, to Anthony Sadleir, Esq; chief and council of Masulipatam.

Gentlemen,

Since the receipt of your letter without date, in which you acknowledge receiving my letters of the 8th and 11th instant, I have been half way between Ellore and Rajahmundry, to review the remains of the first Circar battalion; from which I have selected two companies, that are ordered to Akkerapilly, and the residue sent to Samulcotah, with two three pounders, under the command of lieut. Archibald Brown, to calm the minds of the inhabitants of the adjacent country.

---

* Under a most excellent officer, the sick men of the battalion who were capable of using their arms, defeated the enemy, although they were strongly posted, and secured the country.

From Ellore I went to Condapilly, at which place, and on the way to it, the ſtrength of the party at Combamet was variouſly reported; but all agree that there is a force drawing towards our country from Hydrabad; and that Fauzel beg Chan is expected ſoon at Combamet.

I therefore propoſe that the troops ſhould march to Bezoara, to be ready to oppoſe thoſe that have the appearance of threatening us. During the rains, captain Bridges's battalion may be in the barracks at Condapilly; a battalion, and part of the artillery, may find ſhelter at Bezoara, and the remainder at Akkerapilly, with another battalion. Akkerapilly is twenty miles from Condapilly, and ſixteen from Bezoara, upon the high road that leads from the weſtward to Ellore. By this diſpoſition the troops will be enabled to aſſemble in a few hours, ſhould the diſtrict be invaded from Combamet, or from the other ſide of the Kiſtna. Every other part on this ſide of the Kiſtna is, to all appearance, ſecure.

I beg that you will be pleaſed to mention the number of ſepoys that you want for revenue ſervice, and the places where they are to go. It is true that all abſentees were ordered to join their battalions, but many cannot be found, which will always be the caſe, when ſepoys are employed ſo deſtructive to diſcipline, and prejudicial to the farmer. I ſhall, in future, take all the care that lays in my power, that ſepoys are not employed, excepting on the company's ſervice, becauſe I am well acquainted that heretofore many of thoſe reported on revenue ſervice, were on the buſineſs of individuals.

To explain what I meant by cantooning troops, it may be neceſſary to inform you, that, to the ſouthward, it has been cuſtomary to quarter them in villages, which, in general, is called cantooning them. It was not my intention to put the company to the expence of building barracks. Some better covering than a tent will be neceſſary

cessary during the monsoon, which may be easily furnished by the temporary inconvenience of some villagers, who may, for the time, be accommodated by their friends.

I have the honour, &c.

Richard Mathews.

Camp, Sept. 18, 1778.

The Chief and Council of Masulipatam, to Major Mathews.

Sir,

We addressed a letter to you on the 12th instant, to which we have received no other reply than an acknowledgment from captain Powell of its being come to hand; and that in a few days it should be answered.

There were some particulars in the above letter, that might have been, we judge, immediately replied to; and there was scarcely any, with respect to which, a delay of this kind could not but be attended with inconvenience, and obstruct the course of public business.

We shall point out one or two instances wherein the inconvenience above-mentioned has been sensibly felt; and we trust that the bare mention of this matter will be sufficient to induce you to observe such a conduct in future as may save us the trouble of any further remarks of this kind.

Our chief, on the receipt of the late dispatch from the honourable the select committee, wished to apprise Basili Jung's manager in the Guntoor Circar, of their pacific intentions towards their master, so long as a proper caution was observed, respecting the movements of Mr. Lally: but this would have been altogether improper, until we could at the same time inform him with certainty that the troops were all entirely withdrawn, and had repassed the Kistna; a circumstance

stance regarding which we have not yet any authentic information:* and of courfe the above communication with the Naib of Bafili Jung, fo proper at this juncture, is ftill prevented.

The other inftance we fhall point out, regards the Peddapore and Pettipore countries. The manager of the Zemindar of it has applied fome time fince for relief. He has lately renewed his applications; but your anfwer was wanted to enable us to come to fome refolution on this fubject; and this being delayed, we are ftill prevented from giving them any fatisfaction. The inconvenience to us from that part of your conduct above remarked upon, will appear fufficiently from the foregoing inftances. We pafs now, therefore, to other matters.

By report we learn that captain Bridges was yefterday within four cofs of this place; and that lieutenant Meek is in the command of Condapilly. What has been done concerning the poft at Vantapollam, whether it is occupied as before, or whether the company of fepoys be withdrawn, we are totally unacquainted. We cannot but confider this want of communication on your part as in fome degree a neglect of the orders you have lately received from the honourable felect committee, a copy of which has been forwarded to us; and it obliges us to reprefent the fame that it may in future be rectified.

A Hircar, who is lately come in, has informed our chief, he was prefent at Guntoor when fome people come from you to the manager of that country.† This interference with the country government, in any

---

* Not true. The chief having wrote to the Naib the 29th or 30th of Auguft. See the letter, p. 164.

† What they call interference in the country government, was no more than a letter to the manager of Guntoor, requefting that he would order all the fepoys belonging to the company, who were dragooning his province, to join their corps; and telling him that it was contrary to the orders of the company that their fepoys were fo employed.—See his anfwer in the Appendix, dated Sept. 6.

any public concerns, is entirely out of your line, and must be productive of bad consequences. The inconvenience to affairs, arising from such a double intercourse, is too manifest to need enlarging upon it, will be sufficient to observe, that it must end in throwing all business into confusion, as it will be impossible for those with whom we have to treat, to know which of us they are to rely upon; nor can any consistency of conduct be preserved by us in such a case: whenever you may have public business, in which the country powers are concerned, the chief and council ought to be the channel of it. As a conduct of this kind has never heretofore been allowed to your predecessors, and, we are persuaded, be countenanced by our superiors, we hope no further occasion will be given us to remonstrate against it. We wish to be favoured with your speedy answer, both to this and our last.

   We are, &c.

           Anth. Sadleir,
           James Hodges,
           Thomas Barnard.

Masulipatam, Sept. 18, 1778.

  Major Mathews, to Anthony Sadleir, Esq; chief and council of Masulipatam.

  Gentlemen,

Your letter of the 18th I received, after I had dispatched to you a letter of the same date, in which every necessary part of your letter of no date was replied to. Upon the 13th instant I received that letter, which did not then appear to me as requiring an immediate reply. I was then on the point of going to review the first Circar battalion at, or near Rajamundry, and desired captain Powell to acquaint you of my going to Ellore, and that upon my return you should have an answer, which answer you may have received in due time;

time; and, I hope, hath proved satisfactory. In the mean while I have had it view to secure this district, as far as the united efforts of so small a party can effect. And I make no doubt, since harmony has been so strongly recommended, but that I shall meet with your assistance, most heartily, in all kinds of public service.

I request you to call to mind that my life and profession hath been active, your's of the closet; and I have not leisure, or abilities, to write volumes upon trifles. My time may be better employed in serving essentially the honourable company; every thing, that is necessary, you shall be informed of, other matters are not worth recording.

You say that you will point out two instances wherein inconveniencies have been felt by my not having immediately replied to your letter, *viz.*

1st, " Our chief, on receipt of the late dispatch from the honourable select committee wished to apprise Basalat Jung's manager in the Guntoor Circar of their pacific intentions towards his master, so long as a proper caution was observed respecting the movement of Mr. Lallly; but this would have been altogether improper, until we could at the same time inform him, with certainty, that the troops were all entirely withdrawn, and had repassed the Kistna; a circumstance regarding which we have not yet any authentic information, and of course the above communication with the Naib of Basalat Jung, so proper at this juncture, is still prevented."

To this I need only say, that I wrote to you on the 12th instant; the following is a copy.

" I send you an extract of a letter that I have received from the honourable select committee, dated Sept. 6, 1778."

" As we do not find by the latest intelligence we have received, that Mr. Lally is moving from Adoni, we are of opinion, that it is

un-

unneceſſary to make any detachments from your force at preſent, as it may give much alarm to the inhabitants, and injure the collection of the revenues; we deſire, therefore, that you will fix your camp in ſome proper ſituation for the ſecurity of the diſtrict, and not move any troops towards the Guntoor Circar, without further orders, or without the concurrence of the chief and council of Maſulipatam."

" I have, in conſequence of the foregoing, ſent orders to captain James Powell, to re-croſs the Kiſtna, with all the troops of this diſtrict, that are now to the ſouthward of the Kiſtna.

This will ſhew that, conformably to orders, all the troops were directed to re-croſs the river. Captain Powell's return was immediate; captain Bridges arrived yeſterday at one o'clock; and the two companies of the 7th Carnatic battalion will be over to-morrow or next day. I have alſo ordered that the five boats be taken to Maſulipatam. Thus every offenſive and defenſive appearance are removed, and the orders of the honourable ſelect committee, which were in this point agreeable to your ſentiments, executed in the ſtricteſt and moſt expeditious manner. You could not be informed of the return of the troops until they did return; and they are not at this time all over. But this matter was no " delay to your acquainting the Naib of Baſalat Jung of the pacific intentions of the honourable ſelect committee." The letter from your chief to him, (ſee p. 104.) copy of which you honoured me with, dated the 30th of Auguſt, was ſufficiently clear.

2d, The ſecond inſtance of inconvenience is anſwered by my letter of the 18th, which informs you, that the remains of ſix companies of the firſt Circar battalion, and two three pounders, under the command of lieutenant Archibald Brown, were gone to Samulcotah; and he hath my orders for the ſecurity of the country.

I have heard that Rajanah Dourah, of whom the Peddapore manager complains, had retired from Rutlapundah, in conſequence of

R   his

his father's releafe. But this may not be true; however, in your letter of no date, you agreed with me, that it was prudent to wait for the healthy feafon, and not rifque the lives of any troops at this time among the hills, that at this period, and for three months to come, are almoft certain death to Europeans, and to all others not natives of the climate.

Lieutenant Meek from the village of Yentapollam, joined captain Bridges many days ago at Baumpattah. All the troops being ordered to re-crofs the river, there could not be any left without a frefh caufe; nor do I think it prudent to rifque a fmall party at fuch a diftance. Yentapollam is an open village. I have heard that when lieutenant Meek was ftationed there, he had for fome time only fourteen men; Enfign Bowfer a lefs number, the reft of the company being difperfed about the country. I fancy that thefe are the fepoys to which you allude, when you are pleafed to fay, in your letter of no date, "The utmoft care has always been taken by us not to employ fepoys unneceffarily; we removed many previous to your arrival, and had it at the fame time under deliberation to withdraw them all; but the neceffity of the fervice would not allow of it." The only fepoys that were removed, in fuch a courfe as to rejoin their corps, were thefe abfentees of lieutenant Meek's; and this recall was performed a few days before my arrival at Mafulipatam.

I inclofe you copies of two letters that I fent to Balalat Jung's manager, Rajah Bahauder, one of which your chief's Hircar has given fuch true information of; and, in reply to what you are pleafed to urge, muft confefs that the deftructive war which threatens us on all fides,* will, I am apprehenfive, prevent me from obferving
the

---

* I appeal to all military men, if it be not impoffible for a commanding officer to fecure a province from infult, when he is deprived of the means of guarding againft a fudden attack. If he is debarred from procuring intelligence, he at all times lays expofed

the channel of communication with country powers that you so earnestly recommend.

Before I conclude, I must beg leave to assure you, that it is my wish the service of our country may be conducted by the military and civil powers in union, concord, and harmony; for without this perfect agreement, the honourable company's affairs, which I have seen to flourish nineteen years, may be so much prejudiced, that we may be forced to dance to jarring sounds our ears have been unacquainted with in India since the French were drove from before Madras.

I have the honour, &c.

Richard Mathews.

Camp, Sept. 18, 1778.

The Chief and Council of Masulipatam, to Major Mathews.

Sir,

We have received your late letters, two under date the 12th, and one under date the 18th instant. The latter is in answer to ours of the 12th, and we are sorry to observe to you, that it is by no means satisfactory, not to mention the delay that has happened in favouring us with this reply, for which we cannot perceive any good reason in what you have communicated, there are other circumstances which require our notice.

You have not yet told us what has been done with the party before stationed at Vantipollam, whether that post be still occupied, or has been abandoned. In our letter we recommended the continuing a party at this post.

---

posed to surprise. It seems that the chief and council would wish that the senior military officer was deaf and blind.

But the honourable company's standing order of 1714, explained in March 1769, and further explained in November 1769, allows the commanding officer greater latitude. See appendix.

What force you have kept at Condapilly, and who may have been in the command of it, are circumstances that have been and continue equally unknown to us; the same, with respect to captain Lane's battalion, of which no return has yet been sent, although it should have been done as soon as it conveniently might after the arrival in these districts.

*The neglecting, for so many days after we had required it, to return the sepoys to their stations, on the revenue service, is likewise very exceptionable.

It is possible we may misapprehend the sense of what has been written us by our superiors: but as we cannot reconcile what we understand from their orders, with such conduct on your part, it obliges us to have recourse to them for a further explanation. We shall, therefore, transmit a copy of all the correspondence that has passed between us since the receipt of their late dispatches, for their pleasure to be known upon it.

We proceed to the subject of the arrangements of the troops in cantoonments, as proposed in our letter of the 18th. We do not see any good reason for altering our former opinions, already communicated, by stationing the troops as we then proposed, one battalion at Condapilly, one with the artillery at Ellore, another in addition to the one we now have at this place, and returning the two companies of captain Lane's battalion, now at Akkerapilly, to their corps at Samulcotah, we think more than one advantage will be gained, the detached parties of captain Powell's battalion may be relieved, and the battalion kept complete.

The

---

* They neglected to mention the places where the sepoys were to go, and the particular business they were employed upon. See the company's orders on this head, p. 1. paragraph 54. The number of sepoys that the chief and council required, did not amount to a twentieth part of what were dispersed in the province before my arrival.

The troops, as before-mentioned to you, will be lodged in comfortable and healthy quarters. The expence of Batta, and some other field charges, in part, be avoided. We beg leave to observe here, that the diminishing, in any particular, so heavy a load of expence, as our honourable employers are now burthened with by the charges of the war, ought, we think, to be an object of attention; and lastly, the country be freed for a time from the apprehensions that will always attend the movement of troops.

We cannot concur with you in the opinion you express of the little inconvenience that would be occasioned by quartering troops upon the villages. In our opinion you treat this matter too lightly; it appears to us that in so inclement a season, as that of the Monsoon in this country, the inhabitants must be exceedingly distressed by such a measure, and it would serve besides to keep up the present alarm; whilst good quarters, therefore, may be had for the troops' without any oppression of the inhabitants, we think the measure ought not to be adopted.

We do not at all apprehend immediate danger from the quarters you have pointed our attention to. If the Soubah should ever form the project of invading the country, he will not attempt it with so inconsiderable a force as that which is assembled in the Combamet country, and we apprehend our chief attention for the present should be directed to the preservation of tranquility in these parts: that the cultivation may go on and the course of other business may not be interrupted, we have now offered you our sentiments on this matter; had we neglected to do so, we should not have fulfilled our duty. We rest it with you to act, as in your opinion will best correspond with the instructions you have received from the honourable select committee, and be most conducive to the interest of our honourable employers; for these are the only objects about which we are at any time solicitous.

We

We send you inclosed a list of stations, and the number of sepoys that are to be sent to them, so much time having been already lost in remanding them. We request they may be ordered away without delay.

Since we wrote the above, we have received your letter under date the 18th.* Such part of it as requires any notice shall be duly attended to, a copy of the letter itself goes a number in our packet of this evening. We do not perceive any thing in it that tends at all to weaken the force of our reasoning, with respect to the arrangements proposed by you in this letter.

We are, &c.

Anth. Sadleir,
James Hodges,
Thomas Barnard.

Masulipatam, Sept. 20, 1778.

Major Mathews, to Anthony Sadleir, Esq; chief and council of Masulipatam.

Gentlemen,

One of my people is this instant arrived, he says, from Adoni. He brings information, that Mr. Lally, with all his forces, and the greatest part of Basalat Jung's cavalry, have left Adoni, and marched to the southward. It was reported, that they were going against a tributary Zemindar.

I have the honour to be, &c.

Richard Mathews.

Camp, Sept. 20, 1778.

Major

* A mistake; it was dated the 19th.

Major Mathews, to Anthony Sadleir, Esq; chief and council of Masulipatam.

Gentlemen,

I have the pleasure of inclosing two indents for stores, which I request of you to comply with as soon, and as far, as lays in your power.

I have the honour, &c.

Richard Mathews.

Camp, Sept. 21, 1778.

Major Mathews, to Anthony Sadleir, Esq; chief and council of Masulipatam.

Gentlemen,

I have received your letter of the 20th instant. Concerning Yentapollam and Condapilly you were informed the 27th of August. I have not received a return or present state of captain Lane's battalion.

The sepoys for revenue-service have been sent, as soon as as you informed me to what place they were to go. You neglected this; as also to inform me to whom they were to be sent, and the particular business they were to be employed upon. I have given them directions, to do, for the company's service, whatever the manager of the place they are ordered to, requires, and not to take any batta from the village people.

I am very clear, in respect to the orders of the honourable select committee, and shall obey them in every particular. The preservation of the troops, forces me, in some measure, to deviate from them, which may, I hope, be rectified, without danger to the service.

Bad

Bad quarters, unwholesome water, and the high price of wood, are among the inconveniencies that sepoys labour under in Masulipatam. The unnecessary duty also prevents them being brought to any order. These circumstances cause good men to decline offering their service for battalions stationed in the fort. The quarters for officers are a disgrace to the honourable company, whose wish is, that their officers be accommodated like gentlemen; and that there should not be such a shameful distinction as appears in the houses allotted for the military and civil: the latter are well provided, and their houses in good repair: the quarters of the former are not proof against the weather, and are little better than hogsties. The barracks for the sepoys are only sufficient for the number of men now in garrison, and, as the fort is not in any danger, the present garrison is sufficient for the security of it, and therefore a reinforcement, at this time, unnecessary. I have ordered captain Powell's battalion, and captain Johnstone's, with the major part of the artillery and stores, to Ellore. Captain Bridges goes to Condapilly.

A detachment of two companies of the first Circar battalion, three select picquets, and two six-pounders, will be fixed at Bezwara, ready to move at a moment's warning. Every thing for that purpose should be kept ready with this party, such as draught bullocks, lascars, and artificers; all other extras may be discharged.

As you seem very earnest about the village of Yantapollam, I have, though it is attended with great risk, sent to that place lieutenant Abbot, and two companies of the 7th Carnatic battalion, with orders, in case of the approach of a superior party from Lally's camp, or of Basalat Jung's troops, to retreat, in time, to Ongole.

Lally's march is confirmed by several reports, but the way he is gone, not perfectly known. It is still supposed, that he will come to the northward, after the Desary feast.

Rajah

Rajah Bahader is very busy in preparing military stores, which he sends to Innacundah.

No particular news from Combamet.

I have the honour to be, &c.

Richard Mathews.

Camp, Sept. 22, 1778.

The Chief and Council of Masulipatam, to Major Mathews.

Sir,

We have received the following letters from you, *viz.* two under date the 21st, and one under date the 22d inst.

The indent inclosed in one of the former has been complied with, as far as the situation of our stores will admit. The articles were dispatched from hence yesterday. We beg to be informed concerning the deficiency in this supply of what you indented for, whether it be so important as that you wish to have it supplied, if our stores cannot afford what may be wanted, from the presidency.

We go on to reply to your letter of the 22d inst. A copy of it has been transmitted to the honourable the president and council of the select committee; to their determination upon the merits of it, both as it may respect you and ourselves, we chearfully submit. There is one point, however, in this letter, upon which, although we did, in our last, express our intention of abiding by your judgment, yet the explicit approbation which has since been communicated to us of our conduct in all respects, implying the consent of the honourable the select committee to what we urged on these points, which were explained at the same time, we have resolved thereupon, as abovesaid, to our former intention, to enforce our opinion in this particular, meaning, if you should disapprove of what we require, to take the responsibility of the measure entirely on ourselves.

The accompanying extract from the letter we yesterday received from the honourable the select committee, which we now send you, by their order, will satisfy you that we have their authority for so doing.

The present strength of the garrison will appear to you from this morning's return, a copy of which we now inclose. We are of opinion the place is very insufficiently guarded by such a strength; and further, we see no reason why, at a time the other battalions are not out on actual service, the troops in this place should be unnecessarily harrassed.

The objections you have made against sending another battalion hither, have been weighed, and we think the ballance still more inclines in favour of our opinion.

We must therefore require of you, to send to this place an immediate and considerable augmentation of the force now in garrison, from any part where you think it can be best spared.

Concerning the detachments you have stationed at Bezoara, we have consulted the honourable the president and select committee thereon; as soon as their pleasure is known, it will be communicated.

We are, &c.

Anthony Sadleir,
James Hodges,
Thomas Barnard.

Masulipatam, Sept. 25, 1778.

Extract

Extract of a letter from the honourable the president and select committee, dated Sept. 19, 1778.

We hope our last letter to Major Mathews will have, in a great degree, if not entirely, removed all cause of disagreement, by impressing him with a due sense of his improper conduct towards you, and disposing him hereafter to act with that deference which he owes to your authority, in all matters which do not come within the detail of military operations; for it is our meaning that every thing, which regards the policy and revenue of the country, shall be totally under your direction, and that you shall have power, as far as may be consistent with our general instructions, to change the object of military operation, whenever you may think it necessary, by requisition to the commanding officer, first consulting him, however, if it can be done without delay or inconvenience to the public service.

Having said thus much, it were unnecessary to pass any opinion on Major Mathews's conduct, respecting Yencanah Doorah, further than may be proper to shew our total disapprobation of it; the confinement of this man was an act of the chief and council, confirmed and approved by this government; Major Mathews should have had no power over this man, further than to guard him as a prisoner, at the will of those by whom he was confined; but the setting him at liberty, in the manner he appears to have done, and upon so weak a plea, was an exertion of authority which nothing can justify.

We cannot quit this subject without censuring the want of respect shewn to your board, in the letter written by Major Mathews, particularly in that passage wherein Rajanah Doorah is desired to dismiss his people, and "wait the justice of the expected chief, Mr. Cotsford. These last words imply a strong and unmerited reflection upon the justice of your board, and in that light are very exceptionable. We muſt alſo notice the inconſiſtency of Major Mathews's conduct in this place. He firſt deſires Rajanah-dourah to wait the juſtice of the expected chief, " who, he makes no doubt, will releaſe his father ;"* and, in the next paragraph, tells you that he has thought proper himſelf to ſet him at liberty, without aſſigning any new reaſon for this extraordinary meaſure. But what ſtrikes us more forcibly than any thing we have mentioned, is, the impropriety of Major Mathews's writing at all to Rajanah-dourah upon the ſubject.

The ſame principles which have led to the diſapprobation of almoſt the whole of Major Mathews's conduct towards you, will not allow us to paſs over the inſult contained in the orders, of which you have tranſmitted us a copy. The recall of the ſepoys from the revenue ſervice, in oppoſition to your board, was a very unwarrantable meaſure; but the publication of the order, wherein he ſpeaks of their being abſent on pretence of revenue ſervice, ſtampt the proceedings with a degree of inſult, beyond every thing we could have conceived from the expectations we had formed of Major Mathews's prudence. We alſo much diſapprove of the order being iſſued in your garriſon, without your conſent, and direct that, in future, no garriſon order whatſoever be publiſhed, until it has received your ſanction.

We

---

* The ſelect committee make no allowance for time and other circumſtances. Major Mathews was not guilty of any inconſiſtence. The letter to Rajanah-dourah, wherein Mr. Cotsford was mentioned, was ſent away the 25th of Auguſt, at which time I knew nothing of Yencanah-dourah, and could not have conceived that the chief and council would have kept priſoners a decrepit old man, and a poor woman, for the benefit of the honourable company. Captain Powell did not arrive till the 3d of September, on which day I conſulted him on what was proper to be done with the priſoners, and he agreed with me, that humanity, and the intereſt of the company, demanded their immediate releaſe.

We desire that you will furnish Major Mathews with an extract of this letter, and we hope the sentiments we have expressed on his conduct will have the desired effect, by putting an end to all subjects of difference, which serve only to create animosity, and to deprive us altogether of those services which we expected from the appointment of Major Mathews to the command of the troops in your district.

A true copy.

Thomas Barnard, Secretary.

Major Mathews, to Anthony Sadleir, Esq; chief and council of Masulipatam.

Gentlemen,

In consequence of your request, under date the 25th instant, I have *ordered captain Thomas Bridges to take upon him the charge of the troops in Masulipatam, (there not being a captain of infantry in garrison) and have given directions for two companies of his sepoys to march from Condapilly to Masulipatam. Upon their arrival I request that the company of recruits of captain Johnstone's battalion be ordered to Ellore, that they may be disciplined under the eye of their captain.

I have the honour to be, &c.

Richard Mathews.

Bezwara, Sept. 26, 1778. Major

Fort St. George, Nov. 15, 1777.

* G. O. Colonel Braithwaite appointed to command the fort and garrison at Masulipatam.

By the above extract of General Orders, issued by the Governor and Council of Madras, any person who understands the rules of service, or the signification of words, would conclude, that colonel Braithwaite had charge of the garrison and fort. He had neither. The charge of both was lodged in the hands of the chief civil servant, notwithstanding the orders of the honourable company to the contrary. Col. Braithwaite had not authority to regulate any part of the garrison duty, or had any honourable charge. He, in fact, only received the reports, &c. after the chief, who had usurped the military authority.

Major Mathews, to Anthony Sadleir, Esq; chief and council of Masulipatam.

Gentlemen,

I have the pleasure of informing you of my arrival at Ellore. At Bezwara I was under the necessity of borrowing a few houses for the use of the officers. The inhabitants will only have to complain of the temporary inconvenience, as the gentlemen will take care not to injure their quarters.

I have the honour, &c.

Richard Mathews.

Ellore, Sept. 28, 1778.

Major Mathews, to Anthony Sadleir, Esq; Chief and Council of Masulipatam.

Gentlemen,

*Herewith you will receive three men, their names, Shiach Gee, Fukier Mahomed, and Maura Saheb. They have been prisoners near twelve years; and as it may be proper, by this time, to come to some determination respecting their fate, I beg leave to recommend them to your notice.

I am, &c.

Richard Mathews.

Ellore, Oct. 2, 1778.

The

* This letter was sent by the Havaldar of the guard, for him to deliver to Mr. Sadleir.

The Chief and Council of Mafulipatam, to Major Mathews, commanding the troops in the Mafulipatam diftrict, or officer commanding at Ellore.

Sir,

*Mr. Weftcott having reprefented, that in getting the ftores removed from Samulcotah, he fhall want the affiftance of a conductor, we require that you will order ferjeant Woodford to attend him accordingly, who is to remain under the directions of Mr. Weftcott, fo long as Mr. Weftcott fhall have occafion to detain him.

We are, &c.

Anth. Sadleir,
James Hodges,
Thomas Barnard.

Mafulipatam, Oct. 2, 1778.

Major Mathews, to Anthony Sadleir, Efq; chief and council of Mafulipatam.

Gentlemen,

Under charge of a Havaldar and fix fepoys, I have this day fent three men, who have been prifoners at Ellore for twelve years. I have directed the Havaldar to deliver them to you, to be difpofed of as you think proper.

By a letter I received this morning from lieutenant Brown, I fuppofe he will march with two three pounders, and all the men of the firft Circar battalion that were fit for duty, towards Routlapundy, as the manager for Timrauze was urgent for affiftance to relieve that fort.

I fend

---

* A Mr. Lavallé was conductor, Woodford was not; therefore, the chief and council named and required the wrong perfon.

I send you copies of two letters that I received from Rajanahdourah, that you may take such measures as you think proper. I shall not make any reply to them.

Captain Thomas Lane is ordered to join that part of his battalion now under lieutenant Brown. He has orders to act for the security of the Peddapore, and Pettipore countries, and not to go among the hills at this unhealthy season; except by a sudden incursion he may have an opportunity of gaining a good advantage over the enemy. Captain Lane will also pay attention to the port of Coringy, and to every part near him.

Two of my Hircars say, that Lally is again at Adoni; probably he may not have moved from thence; but for such contradictory intelligence I cannot be accountable. It is reported that he will come to Guntoor after the Desarey feast.

Fauzel beg Chan is laying in great quantities of provisions of all kinds at Combamet: and it is expected that a considerable force will march to that place from Hydrabad after the Desarey feast.

I have the honour, &c.

Richard Mathews.

Ellore, Oct. 2, 1778.

The Chief and Council of Masulipatam, to Major Matthews, commanding the troops in the Masulipatam district, or, commanding officer at Ellore.

Sir,

The salt farmer, Mr. Statham, has applied to us for the assistance of some sepoys to escort some parties of Lombardy people to his salt pans at Ponraca, whither they were prevented from going, by difficulties raised in the countries through which they have to pass, on the subject of the duties to be paid. We require, therefore, that a
Havaldar

Havaldar and twelve sepoys be immediately sent to Aukanapillee, situate not far from Noozeed, when they are to follow the directions of Chandriah, the agent of Mr. Statham. The sepoys are no otherwise to interfere than by preventing the exaction of larger customs, than the Cowle of our chief allows: copy of this Cowle is lodged with Mr. Statham's agent.

We send inclosed a letter to be delivered by the Havaldar to the abovementioned Chandriah.

We are, &c.

Anth. Sadleir,
James Hodges,
Thomas Barnard.

Masulipatam, Oct. 3, 1778.

Major Mathews, to Anthony Sadleir, Esq; chief and council of Masulipatam.

Gentlemen,

I have received your letters of the 2d and 3d instant. The officer at Samulcotah has directions to give every assistance to those employed in removing the stores, so that it will be unnecessary sending Woodford, especially as he may be much wanted with the troops should they take the field.

A Havaldar and twelve sepoys are sent to assist Mr. Statham's servants to escort the Lombardy people.

I have the honour to be, &c.

Richard Mathews.

Ellore, Oct. 4, 1778.

The Chief and Council of Mafulipatam, to Major Mathews.

Sir,

We have received your letters of the following date, *viz.* of the 26th, 28th ult. two of the 2d, one of the 3d, and another of the 4th inftant.

We at prefent only reply to your laft letter, under date the 4th inftant; the others may require further anfwer. We are forry that you fhould oblige us to repeat the requifition we therein made, and lay us under the difagreeable neceffity of reminding you of the command of our fuperiors, which were made known to you in their letter under date the 6th ult. namely, that our requifitions are to be implicitly obeyed. We do then, now, again require of you, to order ferjeant Woodford, the conductor of ftores, to go immediately to Samulcotah, there to remain under the directions of Mr. Weftcott, until the removal of the ftores from that place be completed, or he be recalled. We defire that this requifition be immediately complied with, meaning to charge ourfelves with every confequence thereof.

We are, &c.

Anth. Sadleir.
James Hodges.
Thomas Barnard.

Mafulipatam, Oct. 5, 1778.

The Chief and Council of Mafulipatam, to Major Mathews.

Sir,

We before acknowledged the receipt of your letter, under date the 2d inftant, in ours to you of the 5th inftant; we now proceed to reply thereto.

There would have been a greater propriety in advifing us, before you proceeded further, of the perfons you have fent to this place being

being confined at Ellore, than in ordering them hither without any proper authority for so doing. They were directed, as we judge, to be kept at the above place, by order of this government, and ought not to have been moved, before the sanction of it to such an act had been previously obtained; at least, without great and evident necessity. These prisoners being now here, we shall not order them back. We desire, however, that you will please to enquire of the persons in whose custody you found them, what crimes they were charged with, on which they may have been committed to prison; as it will be difficult to trace the matter to its source in our records.

Concerning Rajanah-dourah, we have searched our records for the particulars relative to him, and we find that it was determined long ago by the superior board, that he merited exemplary punishment, having been guilty of rebellion and murder, his country was ordered to be sequestered, and his person, wherever he could be found, to be seized, that it might receive the punishment due to his crimes; such as the superior board might command to be inflicted. This resolution remains still in force; under such circumstances, therefore, nothing, we think, but unconditional submission to the authority of government, can possibly be admitted; and we communicate this opinion, as well as the other circumstances, that they may serve in this point, for the rule of your conduct.

Respecting the march of lieutenant Brown, having no intelligence whatever from that part of the country where he is, neither from him, nor from the Peddapore manager, we can be no judges of the occasion for it: we did not know of your having issued any orders, which might, upon an emergency, justify lieutenant Brown in taking the field.

We are, &c.

Anth. Sadleir,
James Hodges,
Thomas Barnard.

Masulipatam, Oct. 7, 1778.

Major Mathews, to Anthony Sadleir, Esq; chief and council of Masulipatam.

Gentlemen,

I have ordered the *conductor of stores to Samulcotah to assist Mr. Westcott in conveying the artillery and stores from thence.

Inclosed you will receive a paper concerning the prisoners that I sent to you on the 2d instant. It was wrote by the Cutwall's Concicoply, who seems to know more of the matter than any other person.

Lieutenant Brown has been successful in an attack that he made upon some advanced parties of Rajanah-dourah's; and captain Lane writes me, that he purposed on the 7th to give the enemy another Alert; the result of which you shall be informed in due time.

I have the honour, &c.

Richard Mathews.

Ellore, Oct. 11, 1778.

Major Mathews, to Anthony Sadleir, Esq; chief and council of Masulipatam.

Gentlemen,

Inclosed is an indent, which I beg that you will comply with as therein mentioned. The conductor of stores being absent, I have it not in my power to compare the indents that I made to you on the 21st ult. with what was received at Condapilly; but I beg leave to assure you, that at all times I am careful not to apply for articles that are unnecessary. The number of fuzees, that were mentioned, are wanted to complete the select piquets.

In-

---

* Mr. Lavallé, not serjeant Woodford.

Inclosed are extracts of letters from lieutenant Brown and captain Lane, which are sufficient to shew, that Rajanah-dourah cannot be brought to unconditional submission. The nature of the country, being mountainous and woody, the dreadful effects that the climate hath upon our troops, the bravery of the Polygars, and pusillanimity of Timrauze's people, all act against your policy; so that I beg leave to offer it, as my opinion, that as Timrauze is incapable of protecting the Tontapilly district, or to collect the revenues without the powerful assistance of our troops, that he should not be permitted to interfere with it. Let him be circumscribed to his own lands, then he will not need, of armed men, such a number, that may at some time be prejudicial to us. The company's troops are the only force that should be allowed in the Circars. Rajanah-dourah's family should be put in full possession of what we, in fact, cannot keep from them; by which the company's revenue will be increased, and their sepoys kept in health for more material services. You are well acquainted that the value of the Tontapilly country is an object that Timrauze has in view; and the sum he pays the company bears but a small proportion to what he may have received in time of peace. I cannot see any good reason why the company, by whose power he is enabled to collect the rents, should not themselves reap the advantage of the superiority of their arms. Rajanah-dourah will, I suppose, readily pay to the chief and council what Timrauze has agreed to do, and probably make some encrease. He will not be inclined, from the power in him to defend his lands, to make such excuses for non-payments as Timrauze may do, from the repeated invasions of the country by Rajanah-dourah's adherents. Thus the tribute will be more certain, and the company's troops, by being in health and good order, enabled to maintain their fame. Your records may possibly shew the dreadful effects that the hill-country, at different periods, has had upon our officers and sepoys; so much so, that at one

time,

time, out of sixteen companies of sepoys that formed a camp, there were not two hundred men fit for duty.

The under-mentioned extract, from a discerning sensible officer, deserves your attention: from lieutenant Archibald Brown, dated the 6th of October 1778.

"It seems of no consequence our putting them (Timrauze's people) in possession of any post or country; without company's troops they cannot keep it. I have not been able to prevail on any of his people to go out for intelligence; nor has Perry-rauze a bit more influence over them; his people are the most pusilanimous of any I ever saw, and Rajanah-dourah's are by far the bravest. I give you my word, I never saw so much warm work among the hills as I did yesterday morning. Our people were as lively and spirited as could be wished."

I beg your pardon for touching upon a matter that is in your province. But whatever occurs to me that may tend to the benefit of the honourable company's service, I think it my duty to communicate to those who have power to act for the real interest of their employers.

I have taken the liberty to stop a few of the stores, that were ordered from Samulcotah, as, by so doing, it may save the company the expence of sending them from Masulipatam; as soon as I know the exact quantity, I will give a receipt for them.

When I began this letter I did expect that copies of the Extracts would have been ready to-night; but I now find that the sending them must be deferred until to-morrow.

I have the honour to be, &c.

Richard Mathews.

Ellore, Oct. 17, 1778.

Major

Major Mathews, to Anthony Sadlier, Esq; chief and council of Masulipatam.

Gentlemen,

You will herewith receive extracts of letters from lieutenant Archibald Brown, and captain Thomas Lane.

By the last letters from captain Lane, dated the 14th, I am informed that the rains, which had rendered a river impassable, had prevented the return of the detachment to Samulcotah.

I have the honour, &c.

Richard Mathews.

Ellore, Oct. 18, 1778.

Major Mathews, to Anthony Sadleir, Esq; chief and council of Masulipatam.

Gentlemen,

Having received information that the manager for one of the Zemindars of this district had engaged to assist a Zemindar belonging to the Guntoor Circar, against Wassyreddy-ramanah, who is tributary to us, for that part of his lands which are north of the Kistna. And that Chelacauney Juggiah, of Newjure, was assembling men, in order to send them across the Kistna, for the purpose aforementioned. Considering this proceeding of his, who ought to be entirely dependent upon the company, as an unwarrantable step, full of dangerous consequences to our affairs, at this critical time, I have sent an officer and sixty men, to put a stop to their levies. The intelligence I received, and the orders to the officer, also a translation of a letter to Juggiah, are inclosed.

Herewith you will receive the monthly returns.

I have the honour, &c.

Richard Mathews.

Ellore, Oct. 20, 1778.

Major

Major Mathews, to Anthony Sadleir, Esq; chief and council of Mafulipatam.

Gentlemen,

The party I fent to Newjure returned this morning. Inclofed you will have a copy of a letter from Chelacauney Juggiah to me. He has promifed not to go, or fend any armed men, over the Kiftna. You will alfo receive extracts of a letter from captain Lane, dated Oct. 19, by which you will know that Rajanah-dourah returned to the edge of the Peddapore country, to raife contributions. You may be affured that it is impoffible to reduce him to "unconditional fubmiffion." He has too many friends, not only in the Cicacole diftrict, but in this. The Gulgunda and Pettapore people feem much inclined to affift him.

The Havaldar and twelve fepoys, that you, upon the 3d of October, required might be fent to Akkerapilly, to prevent the Zemindar's people taking more from the Lombardy people than what they were permitted by the chief's cowl, have not yet finifhed this bufinefs; although a fingle Peon ought, with the authority of the chief and council, to have had as much effect as was intended by the thirteen men. The Halvadar was nine days at Akkerapilly, waiting the arrival of Chundriah; after which, the chicanery of Juggiah has left the matter undecided. The Shiredars are purpofely kept out of the way, and Juggiah complains that his enemies impofe upon his mafter Nerriah, otherwife Opperrow.

Accompanying is a letter that Juggiah defired me to forward to you.

I have the honour, &c.

Richard Mathews.

The

The Chief and Council of Mafulipatam, to Major Mathews.

Sir,

We have received your letters under date the 17th, 18th, and 20th inftant, together with the accompanying extracts from the letters of lieutenant Brown and captain Lane.

All your correfpondence relative to Rajanah-dourah, when the honourable felect committee receives the copies we now difpatch, will be before them; they will then be equally informed with us; and will be equally enabled to judge, not only of what you have advifed fpecting Rajanah-doorah, but alfo of the propriety of your conduct throughout this bufinefs; in all other refpects, uninformed as *we are*, of the inftructions given to the officers on this fervice, and of all other particulars preceding the march of lieutenant Brown, that, in your or his opinion, made that meafure neceffary, we think we fhould do wrong to offer any judgment upon it at all. As foon as we receive the commands of the felect committee, they fhall be duly communicated.

We have directed your indent to be complied with, and when ready, the feveral things indented for will be difpatched.

We come now to reply to your letter of the 20th inftant, wherein you inform us that you had detached an officer and fixty men, to put a flop to the levies of Chalacuncy Juggiah, of *Noozeed, who was preparing to crofs the Kiftna, to act againft Vaffyreddy Ramanah. We cannot but confider this act, on your part, of fending out a detachment, without our concurrence, which may eventually be obliged to act offenfively, as totally unwarrantable; and confidering how exprefsly fuch conduct has been forbidden by our fuperiors, even repeatedly fo, we muft confefs that it affects us with equal furprize and concern. We think it neceffary, upon this occafion, to recite fome paffages from the commands of the honourable felect com-

* Newjure.

U

committee, both to you and ourselves; wherein they lay down a rule for your conduct, in their letter to you, under date the 6th of September. They use these words: "The chief and council are the persons charged, under us, with the interests and affairs of the company in the Circars; they are left to be the judges when military assistance is necessary, for the purpose of the revenues, or any other service; and are empowered to make requisitions, which, on the part of the commanding officer, are to receive implicit obedience." Again, in the same letter, they afterwards direct, " that you fix your camp in some proper situation for the security of the district, and not move any troops towards the Guntoor Circar, without further orders, or without the concurrence of the chief and council of Masulipatam." In their letter to us, under date the 19th of September, of which you have an extract, they have these words:

" We hope our last letter to Major Mathews will have, in a great degree, if not entirely, removed all cause of disagreement, by impressing him with a due sense of his improper conduct towards you, and disposing him hereafter to act with that deference which he owes to your authority, in all matters which do not come within the detail of military operations; for it is our meaning, that every thing which regards the policy and revenue of the country shall be totally under their directions, &c." By this latter paragraph, your province is plainly and directly limited to the detail only of military operations, and execution thereof; of the occasion for these operations we are as plainly left the sole judges. We do now therefore require of you not to move any troops from their present stations, in any part of these districts, without our concurrence; excepting only such troops as being, by your orders, now out on service, would, by the effect of this requisition, be kept from their proper, and, for the present, their permanent station. And, in the next place, we do require, that all applications to you, from natives, for military assistance, or interference, and all correspondence from them, involving such a subject,

be

be referred to this board, whose province it is to decide upon these matters. We beg leave to observe to you, that in acting in this manner, we by no means wish to abridge your proper authority. The weight of collecting the revenues, and internal government of these countries, rest upon us; and whilst every responsibility of this kind is so placed, the military power must be under our direction; the detail only of its operations remains with you; and we hope you cannot, in any instance, charge us with any invasion of this your province; but, whilst you thus usurp the direction, and have, at the same time, the detail in your hands of military power, there must be an end of all authority.

We hope that Ensign Wilson has already performed the service he was sent upon, and without being obliged to use any violence; but, should he not, we approve of his continuing where he is, until we write you further, unless before that time he should have effected it.

We are, &c.

Anthony Sadleir,
James Hodges,
Thomas Barnard.

Masulipatam, Oct. 22, 1778.

Major Mathews, to Anthony Sadleir, Esq; chief and council of Masulipatam.

Gentlemen,

I have received your letter of the 22d. Your explanation of extracts of letters from the honourable select committee, is too much in your own favour. The regulations from Europe, that has drawn the line between the civil and military powers, do not give you any military authority, much less such as you seem so desirous of exercising: nor doth the sentiments of the honourable select committee,

mittee, or thofe of the commander in chief coincide with yours. The civil government and revenue are placed under your good management, but the defence of the diftrict and forts is the bufinefs of the military. And I beg leave to acquaint you, that I fhall act conformably to this opinion, until fuperior authority directs me to do otherwife.

I have the honour, &c.

Ellore, Oct. 24, 1778.   *Richard Mathews.*

The Chief and Council of Mafulipatam, to Major Mathews.

Sir,

We have received your letter, under date the 22d inftant, with the inclofed Extract from captain Lane's letter, copy of both we now difpatch to the honourable felect committee, to whofe judgment it muft be fubmitted what meafures will be beft to adopt, for the purpofe of reftoring peace in the Peddapore diftricts, and fecuring them from future difturbance. In the mean time, we approve of what captain Lane purpofes in his letter; his defign of moving againft Rajanah-dourah, fhould he appear in the open country, without, however, purfuing him amongft the hills.

We are forry you fhould oblige us fo frequently to animadvert upon your conduct: your remark on the little effect produced by the aid of the fepoys, lately required to protect the falt farmer in his rights, leads us to this obfervation. If the authority of the chief and council be, in fact, reduced fo low, as you reprefent it, that even the aid of a military power to enforce its decrees, it fhould not be able to effect what a fingle Peon, poffeffed therewith when duely in force, ought to accomplifh, we are forry for it: the fault, we hope, does not reft with us; and as we do not perceive in what manner this remark of your's tends to reftore their authority, or to

any

any other good purpose, we must request, for the future, you will keep such opinions to yourself; at least, not give them to us. They are highly disrespectful; and, therefore, contrary to the orders we were instructed to communicate to you. When a requisition is at any time made to you, it is ordered by our superiors, that you should implicitly comply therewith; and when you afterwards interfere therein, excepting an improper use be made of the military aid required, you get entirely out of your province. It is the business of the parties themselves to make the representations communicated in the latter part of your letter; they ought to come directly from them.

   We are, &c.

           Anth. Sadleir,
           James Hodges,
           Thomas Barnard.

Masulipatam, Oct. 25, 1778.

P. S. We have this instant received your letter of the 24th instant; copy thereof goes inclosed to the honourable select committee with your former letters; we can have no other reply to give thereto.

  Major Mathews, to Anthony Sadleir, Esq; chief and council of
          Masulipatam.

 Gentlemen,

I have received advice that the Soubah has taken the field, and expects to be joined by a body of Marattas. It is supposed that he means to act against Fauzel beg Chan. The Soubah's son is, with a part of his father's army, to attack Combamet; from whence this intelligence came.

In your letter of the 2ad, you repeat being uninformed concerning the instructions given to officers who were employed against Rajanah
              dourah

dourah, which assertion gives me much concern; because in all the letters of the undermentioned dates, I have acquainted you of either the orders given, or whatever came to my knowledge worth your attention; and you have acknowledged the receipt of them all.

Viz. the 27th of August, captain Powell to provide for the security of the alarmed inhabitants, &c. The 11th of September. The 18th of September. The 19th of September. The 2d of October, a full account of my orders to captain Lane, which were only a repetition of those given to lieutenant Brown, and agreeable to your own sentiments.

The 11th of October, an account of lieutenant Brown's success. The 17th of October, an account of captain Lane's expedition. The 18th of October, that the rains prevented the return of the detachment to Samulcotah.

Upon the 26th of August, the following orders were given an officer detached on the above service.

" You will march with your detachment to Samulcotah, and from thence attend the motions of Rajanah-dourah of Tontapilly, who, it is reported to me, is preparing to invade our districts, or the country belonging to our tributaries."

" You will do your utmost to protect all those dependent on the company; and you will demand assistance from the people belonging to Peddapore and Pettapore, or any of the Zemindars whose lands are threatened with invasion. Should they fail in giving the necessary assistance, which is so much for their own security, you will acquaint me therewith, and not fail to give me constant and early information of every occurrence; and to observe my orders agreeably to the honourable company's regulations of military service therein laid down for subordinacies."

" You

" You are not to confider the fortrefs of Samulcotah as a defence; but you are to meet the invaders in whatever part may be threatened, for the fecurity of the country. But you are not to go among the hills, which has already been the grave of fo many of our countrymen."

And on the 25th of September the following orders to lieutenant Brown.

" Should not the Peddapore or other countries eaftward of the hills be threatened by Rajanah-dourah, and that he has broke up from before Routlapundah, you will march your detachment into the fort of Samulcotah, and place them in the barracks; but they are to have every thing neceffary for moving at the fhorteft notice."

Upon the 13th of September, lieutenant Brown had inftructions fimilar to thofe iffued the 26th of Auguft.

Upon the 29th of September, I wrote to lieutenant Brown.

"At this unhealthy feafon I would have you confine your operations to the fecurity of the country eaftward of the hills, and not to go amongft them, excepting, if by a fudden incurfion of one day, or two at moft, an advantage might be gained over the enemy by beating up their quarters. This is the fum of the inftructions that I had the pleafure of communicating to you, when we heard that Rajanah-dourah was befieging Routlapundah.

On the firft of October a letter to captain Lane contained thefe words.

" When you was at Ellore, I did myfelf the pleafure of informing you of the general and particular orders that I had given to lieutenant Brown, of which he will acquaint you. This day I received a letter from him, dated the 29th ult. advifing me of his intention to march as the next day, " in order to reftore peace to the country of the

Rajah

Rajah Timrauze, by expelling Rajanah-dourah and his adherents therefrom." It is not my wish that at this unhealthy season the troops should go among the hills, excepting they can effect something very material, and return in two days. We must wait for a more favourable season to expel Rajanah-dourah and his followers from the Tontapilly country. In the mean while, our attention must be, to protect the Peddapore and the Pettapore countries; the latter, it is thought, assists the enemy, of which you will endeavour to obtain certain information, that punishment may follow such a breach of duty."

I think that your recruits cannot be of any service in the field, and that you had better have them all in the fort of Samulcotah.

Should there be a necessity of having any of your people near the hills, you will find Darmarum to be a good situation for the protection of the countries east of the hills. It is ten cofs from Samulcotah, four cofs from Tontapilly, in the mouth of that valley, and two or three cofs from Bendapundy, which is in the entrance of Routlapunda valley. It is high ground, and there is plenty of good water. You will in a few days be enabled to judge what number are necessary to be stationed at that place, or at any other, and recall all that you can to Samulcotah, that you may be enabled to bring your people to some order by the month of January, when we have every reason to expect urgent occasions for all the men we can muster.

" You are to pay attention to the security of the company's country, in general, that is near you, and in particular to the port of Coringy."

By these Extracts you, gentlemen, will perceive that I have paid every possible attention to the parts in question, and that you have received every necessary information, which, to unprejudiced men, will hold me clear of those insinuations you so liberally throw out of my neglect.

Being

Being at the head of the troops, I consider it my duty to keep peace in the Circars. If I had permitted Chelacauney Juggiah to send those men across the Kistna, that he had promised to Monickrow, it might have been attended with bad consequences, and I might have been blamed by you for not preventing it, being situate twenty miles nearer to Newjure than is your residence at Masulipatam. Therefore, I acted as I informed you, and gave you immediate advice thereof. It was a circumstance that would not admit of the delay of writing to you for your concurrence, because it is possible, that before you had determined what to do, his troops might have crossed the river, and entered Basalat Jung's country, to act against one of our tributaries. It is my opinion, that the commanding officer of the honourable company's troops in this district, should have latitude for the defence of it, upon every occasion, and not to be sunk, as you would wish, into a mere Roster-keeper. You attempt to define away all the honourable part of his profession, and would, with much pleasure, leave him the clerk-like occupation of the detail only.

I have received your letter of the 25th. It is certain that Nerriah's, alias Operrow's managers, have not paid proper respect to the chief's cowl, notwithstanding that Chunderiah has had all the aid that you required. But this is not the first time that the country people have refused such obedience. About twelve months ago, captain Powell was obliged to send a Jamadar's party, which were much abused by the then * manager's peons.

My zeal for the service, and regard for justice, induces me to believe, that wherever troops are stationed, the officer commanding should make it his business to afford protection to the inhabitants, and to assist in every thing that tends to the benefit of the company, either for their honour or advantage; especially when required by those

* Mr. Hodges.

those employed by the chief and council, or by any dependent upon them, in their character, as delegates of the president and council of Madras. Such interference, in a good cause, cannot lessen the authority of the chief and council, but serves effectually to uphold and increase it. I am much at a loss to know your meaning, when in the very act of doing my duty, by giving you the necessary information, whereby you may take measures to force Chelacauney Juggiah to pay due and implicit obedience to the chief's cowl, that you are pleased to stile my proceeding "highly disrespectful." I must take the liberty of telling you, that I believe the honourable select committee have not authorized you to pass so unjust a censure. You have, ever since my coming to the Circars, with those orders that the select committee were pleased to honour me, cavilled with, and carped at, every act of mine, right or wrong. However, I shall steadily pursue the line of conduct I have hitherto observed, and, with all due submission, wait the judgment of our superiors upon its merit.

An improper use was on the point of being made by Chundriah, with the guard left to his directions; for, instead of employing them to pass the Lombardy people that were at Akkerapilly, he endeavoured to persuade the Havaldar to go with him to *Mylavaram, one hundred miles from Akkerapilly, towards Combamet; this came to my knowledge, and my interference prevented it; which I fancy to be within the line of my province.

That part of captain Lane's battalion, which was in the Tontapilly country, are returned to Samulcotah.

I have the honour, &c.

Richard Mathews.

Ellore, Oct. 26, 1778.

---

* To force other Lombardy people down to his master's salt-pans.

Major Mathews, to Anthony Sadleir, Esq; chief and council of Masulipatam.

Gentlemen,

Some days ago I was informed, that the inhabitants of two villages had deserted them. Two men from one of the villages came to me, and required fifty sepoys to go and attack the men of the other village. Upon which I told them, that I could not allow of such extremities, but would enquire into the cause of their complaints. I sent a peon, who brought me word that the major part of the inhabitants were in their villages, but that the head men had fled to a village of Opperow's. The next day, I sent to them to know why they had left their habitations; and, by their answer, was much surprized to find that those who had quitted the honourable company's lands, were the head men of several villages belonging to Ellore * Navally. In the evening of the 23d, a letter was left, by a person unknown, with my Dubash's servant, which letter, directed for me, had been *broke open*. It proved to be a petition from the head men, copy of which is inclosed. Upon having this explained, I sent a man to them to hear their complaints, and they returned, by him, another petition (copy inclosed) with a copy of the former, both signed by the head men, or Chowdrys of the several villages in the Ellore Havally. Their complaints are of such a nature, that the credit and justice of the company, as well as the future welfare of their country, are much concerned; also the pretensions of the † Renter Ragojee. For if he has, as is represented, seized all the grain, which not being sufficient, he purposes making them dispose of their cattle and effects; and clearing the old ballances from the produce of the ensuing crop, to answer his demands, ruin must follow.

I have

---

* Lands belonging to the government; *i. e.* company's lands.
† Mr. Westcott's Dubash.

I have no further interfered in this matter than what I relate to you; and such interference I consider myself authorised to do, by my bounden duty to the honourable company.

If you have not any objections, I purpose discharging all the draught bullocks that are now in the service, at Ellore, and to send all the lascars, that are not wanted here, to Masulipatam.

I have the honour, &c.

Richard Mathews.

Ellore, Oct. 28, 1778.

Major Mathews, to Anthony Sadleir, Esq; chief and council of Masulipatam.

Gentlemen,

According to the desire of the head men of the several villages in the Ellore Havally, I sent for one of the Muzemdars, which is one of the three countrymen that the head men mention as their enemies; but, to my surprize, he, Guzzevelly Venhatanarsu, corroborates and confirms all that the petitioners complain of, and which, as it concerns the honour of the company, deserves your serious attention. I shall send for the several head men, and afford them all due protection; and they will, with proper submission, wait the decision of your resolves.

I shall take the liberty of sending to you literal translations of the petitions, that our honourable masters may be duly informed of the several circumstances that I am obliged to make known to you.

I have the honour, &c.

Richard Mathews.

Ellore, Sept. 28, 1778.

The Chief and Council of Masulipatam, to Major Mathews.

Sir,

We have received your letters, under date the 26th and 28th inst. We think it needless to say any thing in reply to the former; copy of it will be laid before the honourable select committee, and with them it will rest to pass a judgment thereon.

We are surprized that you should have troubled us on the subject which was made the occasion of your letter of the 28th; especially after we had, in our last, told you so expressly, that we expected all applications of that nature should come directly to us, and not through the channel of the commanding officer. This perseverance, on your part, in thus unnecessarily forcing your services upon us, makes it necessary to declare to you again, that we will not, in future, take any notice of applications that are so conveyed to us; and that you may be convinced of our purpose fully to adhere to this resolution, we now return the petitions you last sent us inclosed; and should we receive any more in this manner, they must be destroyed.

We approve entirely of your proposal to discharge the draft bullocks, and to send hither the lascars. If any of the artificers could be dismissed, or any other article of expence be reduced, without distressing the service, you have our consent for doing what may be proper therein, and Mr. Westcott is duly informed of this.

We send you a copy of a petition we have received from the *Renter of the Ellore Havally. We request you will please to inform us, what occasion you may have given for the report of your conduct contained therein.

We are, &c.

Anth. Sadleir,
James Hodges,
Thomas Barnard.

Masulipatam, Oct. 31, 1778.

P. S.

* Mr. Westcott's Dubash.

P. S. A copy of the above petition will be sent to-morrow, as it could not be prepared in time to go by this night's Tappy.*

Major Mathews, to Anthony Sadleir, Esq; chief and council of Masulipatam.

Gentlemen,

You will herewith receive a translation of the Petition that the head men of the Ellore Havally sent me; copy of which petition I forwarded to you on the 28th instant.

I am, &c.

Richard Mathews.

Ellore, Oct. 31, 1778.

The Petition of the Chowdrys, belonging to Ellore Havally, to Major Mathews.

You wrote to us to know the reason why we left our villages, because you would wish that justice should be done to us, which to hear

---

* Ragojee's petition is dated the 29th of October; but the following letter from his master will shew, that the petition was sent four or five days before the 27th, which was before I had received the petition from the head men. See the date of it. When the petition came to my hands, I was concerned to see the paymaster mentioned in company with Ragojee, and therefore sent the paper to him, that he might not be ignorant of the complaints. He returned the following answer.

"I have received your note, and thank you for the Gentoo letter you sent me, addressed to you. I have had the letter translated. I am security for the last year's Jemabundy, which was settled by Mr. Pringle, and not by Ragojee, as deposed; as he never yet settled one. If you listen to their stories, or give them a shadow of protracting their time for settling the Jemabundy, nothing can be done. The characters of the inhabitants are well known to the board of Masulipatam, to whom Ragojee has written, four or five days since, and applied for assistance, and he is ready to answer any allegations to the board."

Signed   *George Wykett.*

Dated *Ellore*, Oct. 27, 1778.

hear makes us very glad. We wrote to you a petition yesterday, copy of which we now send by your Gomastah Rajanah. Three or four years ago, the country not producing its usual crops, we suffered great loss, at which the company had the management of the Havally, when we thought that we should get our shares, and our families be preserved in good condition, which induced us to think of taking up money to enable us to go on with the cultivation, and do our endeavours to please the company. Subaram managed the country before Mr. Pringle, and whatever the country produced in Mr. Pringle's time was put under the charge of Ragojee Puntalu. In what he forced us you will see in the following articles.

1st. The renters share of the Paddy he forced us to take at an increased price. The price in the Bazar was three pagodas per putty, and he made us pay him at the rate of pagodas four and a quarter per putty. The loss we are at on this account we expect from him.

2d. The Sauderwarru-kerfu, the Muzemdars people and him should explain to us, which (sundry expences) used to be defrayed by our joint contributions: but so much as is now demanded we never before paid. If you send for the Muzemdar and examine the accounts, you will find how much we have been overcharged, which overcharge should be placed to our credit.

3d. He has made the difference of half a pagoda per putty to us. In the article of measuring the farmers used to have an advantage. The Jemabundy used to be settled as was the Bazar price. Sometimes the price of paddy per putty might be five or six pagodas. By constant usage the farmers used to give the Amuldar half a pagoda as a present; since the management of Ragojee the farmers have not any advantage by the measuring. Supposing the Bazar price might be three pagodas per putty, he charged us more, and said, that the usual custom of giving a pagoda to the Amuldar should be discontinued to them, and that he would receive it. To which we not agree.

4th,

4th. Gramacurſu and Bazaucurſu ſome uſed to be allowed to the renter. He has made new regulations. Whatever he has taken more than uſual, according to the Muzemdar's account, he ſhould return to us.

5th, For the old balance a bond is drawn out in the *paymaſter's name, with intereſt.

It was always cuſtomary, when a bond is made out for balance due by the country people, that intereſt ſhould be mentioned as a matter of form ; but ſuch intereſt, nor any intereſt was never paid. But now Ragojee demands the principal and intereſt, at the rate of three per cent, per month, which he is not entitled to.

In all the above articles we are treated with great injuſtice. Ragojee, by his accounts, wants to get a great deal of money from us, which forces us to fly from our villages, for want of a protector. If we were to remain at our homes, we could not afford to pay the Batta demanded by the people that are ſent to us. We belong to the company, and ſhall be glad of the favour of any gentleman that would hear what we have to ſay, and to do us juſtice. If this cannot be done, we are compelled to ſeek a livelihood in another country. This is the company's country that Ragojee rents. If he gains four thouſand pagodas, he keeps the money; but if, by a failure of the crop he loſes, ‡he is ſtill obliged to pay the company. His renterſhip is only to laſt five or ſix months, after him we know not who will have it. Now the †Colar is full, and it is time to prepare for the Dalvey cultivation ; if this is not done the company muſt not blame us. We have nothing to eat ; our creditors trouble us ; we cannot bear this.

Now the old balance of four years Ragojee wants to be paid in this one year, and has taken away all the grain of the country, the inhabitants ſhare as well as the renters, which he buried in holes; and

---

* Mr. Weſtcott.   ‡ Not the farmer.   † A large lake.

and forced us to give black paddy at pagodas two and three quarters per putty: in this manner he has settled the price and forced a writing from us. These oppressions we cannot live under, and are forced to abandon our villages.

This year he has not told us to prepare to cultivate, nor advanced us any money. We have been at all the expence of cultivation, and now Ragojee wants to have the old balances out of the crop that is now growing. This is another reason why we cannot remain in the company's country.

Three of our countrymen do not agree with us. If you send for them, and put them upon their oath, they will confirm the truth of all the aforementioned particulars.

We are industrious poor farmers; you are a charitable person; the inhabitants of the Circar are the company's children. If you send a Cowl to us by one of your Gomastahs, and one of our three countrymen, and promise to do justice to us, we will go to you; and after you have enquired into the matter, we will be ready to obey your orders, for which we write this petition. You must favour us by sending one of our countrymen and your Gomastah, and then we will go to you. This is what we have to say, and you may use your pleasure.

Signed by the head men, or Chowdrys of the under-mentioned Pergunahs.

Ellore, Dendalure, Cavally, Chauttaperrn, Potanure, Peddapaddu, Poningy, Jallapucuddy, Vuttalum.

Wrote the 25th of October, received the 26th in the Evening.

N. B. The three countrymen alluded to are the Muzemdar, Conicoply, and Dafeepaundeah.

Major Mathews, to Anthony Sadleir, Esq; Chief and Council of Masulipatam.

Gentlemen,

I have received your favour of 31st ult. Whatever I transmit to you, in your public character, as chief and council of Masulipatam, I expect to find recorded; that your masters and mine may be enabled to judge of the merits of their servants: and I request of you to be very careful of the most trifling note, that I shall think proper to send you upon any business relative to the welfare of the company.

When the renter Ragojee, his petition or copy thereof comes to my hand, it shall be answered; but, standing as I do upon firm ground, I laugh at such Asiatic tricks.

The draft bullocks are discharged. The Lascars will remain as they are for a few days.

I go this afternoon for Bezwara, where I shall be ready to receive your commands.

I have the honour to be, &c.

Richard Mathews.

Ellore, Nov. 1, 1778.

The Chief and Council of Masulipatam, to Major Mathews.

Sir,

We have received you letter, under date 1st instant. We shall no otherwise reply thereto than by sending you copy of a letter we now dispatch to the select committee.

We have reason to apprehend that Venhatachalum, renter of Condapilly Havally, who stands indebted in a large sum to the company,

has

has a design of absconding and going off to Heiderabad, to avoid being called to any account for his misconduct as a renter; We do, therefore, require of you to send immediately a proper force of sepoys to Condapilly, and give them orders to seize his person, and bring him to this place; being careful, however, not to treat him with any unnecessary rigour. You will please to give directions, that this may be done with as much secrecy as the thing will admit, lest the man should take an alarm and be enabled to make his escape.

   We are, &c.

             Anth. Sadleir,
             James Hodges,
             Thomas Barnard.

Masulipatam, Nov. 3, 1778.

  Ragojee, to Anthony Sadleir, Esq; chief and council of Masulipatam.

  Gentlemen,

 Since I rented the Havally, the commanding officers of this place not trouble any of my country business.

 Since Major Mathews's arrival here, I have supplied him, the coolies, &c. whatever he wants from my country. I do not know what he thinks; he told his Dubash to find something upon me, about the country business; the dubash send for the inhabitants secretly, and ask them that business, and they tell, if he, Major, can assist and turn the last year's Jummabundy, which was settled by Mr. Pringle, by means of Ragojee, they shall be against me. I do not know what he went and spoke to the Major; the inhabitants are all gone away to Opperrow's country, and send word to the Major, who favoured and wrote them a Cowle, and desired them to write a petition to him, whatever they wants to settle: they did accordingly, and they wrote him the Jummabundy, settled by Mr. Pringle, they
          did

did not like, as alſo mentioned whatever money advanced by the honourable company to them in Subaram's time for the cultivation, they cannot pay that money now; this manner they wrote ſeveral lyes in the petition. Mr. Pringle is making much hurry to collect the cultivation money from the inhabitants, by Major aſſerting, they do not chuſe to pay the cultivation money, nor they will come to me to ſettle the laſt year's Jummabundy.

I was due to the company a great deal money, and alſo to the merchants, therefore, the company muſt pleaſe to favour and give me ſome aſſiſtance, and I will bring the inhabitans from Operrow's country, for to ſettle the Jummabundy, without ſepoys they wont come, nor any buſineſs will go on in the country. Your honour muſt pleaſe to write the Major not to give any aſſiſtance to the inhabitants, nor to trouble any of the country, buſineſs then will go on very well. If the Major make trouble, inhabitants not pay money, and no buſineſs can do; after this manner your honour not make me anſwerable for Kiſtys, and what money I have paid your honour, I hope your honour will conſider if not paid back, I muſt loſe very much, and my family very much ruin. I hope your honour conſider this buſineſs, and

I am, very much reſpect,

Your honours dutiful and humble ſervant,

Ragojee.

Ellore, Oct. 29, 1778.

A true copy. *Thomas Barnard,* Secretary.

Major

Major Mathews, to Anthony Sadleir, Esq; chief and council of Masulipatam.

Gentlemen,

I have received a copy of a petition to you from Ragojee, the nominal renter of the Ellore Havally.

Although I think it beneath me to make any reply to such a heap of forgeries, yet, as I suppose it may be framed to invalidate the testimony of the several head men, who petitioned to me for a redress of their grievances, I shall think my time well employed in endeavouring to obtain justice for the weak and oppressed.

I must take the liberty of observing, that it would better have become your station, when you received copies of the petitions I sent you, to have determined to make the necessary enquiries, than to have attempted to crush such acquittances of duty to our honourable masters, and service to their subjects. It would be bad policy in the sheep to apply to the wolf for protection. It is probable that the petitioners knew the best channel to have their complaints conveyed you, and in this part have succeeded.

I would wish that all commanding officers knew their duty to the honourable company, by protecting the farmers and other inhabitants from injury; and not to sacrifice the real interests of the company for the private purpose of Individuals. I have been told by one officer, that he had heard many complaints against Ragojee, who had reason to apprehend being assassinated, therefore applied for sepoys to be a security to his person. This is a proof that an officer has interfered, and that by some oppressive measures Ragojee had irritated the inhabitants to a degree of frenzy.

I know not of any country Ragojee has of his own, nor that I ever applied to him for Coolies, &c. as a matter of favour. My servants

vants are in monthly pay, and whenever I occasionally employ others, they are regularly paid; a custom not usual in this district.

My Dubash, different from others, has not power to do one single act without my orders: his long and faithful services, on many trying occasions, will induce me to engage my word that he would not presume to take a step without my knowledge and permission. He is merely an interpreter, and not a Director or Manager. He never sent for the inhabitants " secretly," about the Zumabundy, nor were they ever applied to but in the manner I have related to you in my letters of the 28th, 30th, and 31st ult. nor did I interfere any further than as you have been informed. By my absence from *Ellore the field is left open for information of all sorts, and I hope that such will be made as will satisfy the honourable select committee of the injustice done to the inhabitants of Ellore Havally, and to expose the iniquity of the renters and others.

You will be pleased to order him to give proofs of his assertions, and let me know the names of his evidences.

At different times I have received petitions from private people, and from the Tanadars of villages, complaining that their cattle were pressed and employed on the company's business, without being paid any hire, or even Batta for the Coolies. In one is mentioned that three hundred bullocks and buffaloes, and two hundred Coolies were taken twenty-four miles: the owners received no recompence for the damage their cattle had sustained, or for other unavoidable expences that they were at on the road. This is a species of oppression that the honourable company would be much concerned to hear, was frequently practised in their country, and upon their subjects.

You will herewith receive a translation of a letter that I received from the head men of Ellore Havally, which was wrote in consequence

---

* Bezwara is forty miles from Ellore.

quence of my sending the Muzemdar to them, to desire them to go to Ellore, there to wait your orders.

I have the honour to be, &c.

Richard Mathews.

Bezwara, Nov. 3, 1778.

P. S. My Gentoo writer not having arrived from Ellore, I must defer sending a Gentoo copy, of the letter from the head men, until he comes.

Translation of a letter from the Chowdrys, belonging to the Ellore Havally, to Major Mathews, received at Ellore, the 1st of November 1778.

We have received a letter from you with Venkatanarsu the Muzemdar, in which you desire us to go to you, and that you will take care of us according to further orders, which makes us very glad. To-morrow is an unlucky day to go to you. It is the usual custom on these occasions, that the three countrymen should come to us, which we mentioned in our petition; but you only sent Vankatanarsu. If we were to go to you with only Vankatanarsu, it would not be right. When you can settle the business between us and Ragojee Puntalu, the three countrymen should be with us. Upon which account you should send the three countrymen, and your Gomastah, and then we will wait upon you. We hear that Ragojee Puntalu is gone to Masulipatam, it will be, therefore, needless for us to go to Ellore. When Ragojee returns, if you will send to us our three countrymen, and your Gomastah, it will be better. If we were to go to you now, we know not what new regulations Ragojee may bring from Masulipatam. If Ragojee was to come to us at this place, we would not put so much trust in his promises as to go with him to Ellore. We are willing to stay under your protection,

‑tion, and to follow any courſe that you would adviſe us. You muſt not be angry with us, becauſe we have not gone to you upon your ſending for us. We have no other protector; we will, therefore, ſtay here and depend upon you. Until this time Ragojee Puntalu, nor any of his people, have thought proper to ſend for us. We will ſtay in this place until Ragojee Puntalu's return; when he does, he may deſire you to ſend for us; when we receive your letter ſo to do, we will place our dependence upon it; but put no truſt in him. To whom have we to apply. You muſt grant us our requeſt, and after the renters return ſend for us properly.

After Ragojee's return, if he deſires you to ſend for us, it is well; but if he does not, and you ſend for us, we will reſt our cauſe upon you. How to make the neceſſary enquiries into the buſineſs between Ragojee and us, you are well acquainted with; until which time we will go to Vengure, and ſtay there. You muſt not think that this is a common letter. Upon every occaſion we entirely depend upon you, and look upon you as our ſanctuary.

The tranſlation by Snake, at Bezwara, Nov. 3, 1778.

Major Mathews, to Anthony Sadleir, Eſq; chief and council of Maſulipatam.

Gentlemen,

Your letter of the 3d inſtant, with a copy of one to the honourable the ſelect committee I have received, and am happy to find that you have taken the moſt likely ſtep towards putting a ſtop to the evils complained of.

Incloſed you will receive copy of the letter; tranſlation thereof I ſent you in my laſt.

The renter of Condapilly Havally is ſecured, and will be conducted to Maſulipatam as ſoon as poſſible.

Captain

Captain Lane has wrote to me, that fifteen hundred men has joined Peryrauze, near Peddapore, from the Vizagapatam district being sent, it is said, by Venkattyrauze, commandant to Viziaramrauze, to act with Timrauze's people against Rajanah-dourah, who is now in the Tontapilly country. The following is an extract of what I wrote to captain Lane on the subject.

"It is impolitic to permit one of our tributaries to assist another with an armed force, to attack a third, and more especially without leave. The junction that you relate, appears to me very extraordinary, because I know that Rajanah-dourah has been supported by Viziaramrauze; and that the Vizianagarum family wish, and hath really sought the destruction of Timrauze's. You will pay particular attention to what is going forwards, and forbid the people belonging to Venkattyrauze to enter our district on any pretence. The company's troops are at all times the properest, to be employed, to punish the disobedient."

You will be pleased to favour me with your sentiments, that the most prudent measures may be taken on this occasion.

I have the honour, &c.
Richard Mathews.

Bezwara, Nov. 5, 1778.

The Chief and Council of Masulipatam, to Major Mathews.

Sir,

We have received your letter of the 5th instant. You would have received our reply sooner, but that we expected some further explanation on the subject of your letter, from those who might have ordered the party you mention, to enter these districts. We have not, however, received any; and as you are, therefore, equally informed in this matter with ourselves; as you have already, by denying the above party entrance into these countries, adopted a decisive measure,

sure, in doing which, you thought not proper to consult us; and as from all your previous conduct, and particularly in this instance, it appears that you do not admit of the authority we claim in these matters, by vertue of the orders of our superiors, to determine upon them for ourselves in the first instance, and not to follow the lead of others; for these reasons, we decline, until we are further informed on the subject we now write to you, offering any opinion thereon.

We are, &c.

Anthony Sadleir,
James Hodges,
Thomas Barnard.

Masulipatam, Nov. 9, 1778.

Major Mathews, to Anthony Sadleir, Esq; chief and council of Masulipatam.

Gentlemen,

Lieutenant Abbot informs me, that a French ship, with 200 soldiers on board, was seen the 7th instant off Mutapilly.

I do myself the pleasure of acquainting you, that I purpose going to view the coast, from Nizampatam to near Yentapollam.

If you send your commands in a separate pacquet by the Tappal, they will probably come safe to hand.

I have the honour, &c.

Richard Mathews.

Chicacolum, Nov. 11, 1778.

Major Mathews, to Anthony Sadleir, Esq; chief and council of Masulipatam.

Gentlemen,

I have taken the liberty of opening the pacquets from Madras, of the 4th, 5th, 6th, 7th, 8th, 9th, 10th, and 11th. The number of letters taken from each is mentioned on a piece of paper.

The

The vessel that was seen off Mutapilly supposed to be French, was discovered the day before yesterday, in company with a sloop of Baumpetla, standing to the northward.

I have the honour, &c.

Richard Mathews.

Yentapollam, Nov. 17, 1778.

The Chief and Council of Masulipatam, to Major Mathews.

Sir,

We have received your letters, under date the 3d, 5th, 11th and 17th instant. We shall transmit copy of your letter in reply to Ragojee's complaint, to the honourable the select committee; it will rest with them to pass an opinion thereon.

Respecting the ship and vessel cruizing off Baumpetla, and supposed to be French,* we are of opinion, that it will be unnecessary to order troops from these parts to oppose any attempts from them. Captain Barclay has informed us, that he has reinforced lieutenant Abbot with a company from Ongole; and the grenadier companies from the Circars, having been under orders for marching, and to halt at Ongole, so early as the 6th instant, may reasonably be expected to reach that place† as soon as troops that could march from any of the garrisons of this district, upon the receipt of orders from hence.

We inclose copy of a petition from the Tanadar of Bezwara. We desire you will make enquiry into the grounds of his complaint, and take such measures as the result may point out to be proper.

---

* Seven days after receiving the news.

† The did not arrive at Ongole before the 23d of December.

[172]

Although the petition‡ is of an early date, the abuses complained of still continue, and have been repeatedly represented.

We are, &c.

Anth. Sadleir.
James Hodges.
Thomas Barnard.

Masulipatam, Nov. 19, 1778.

Translation of a letter from Calabarga Juggapah, Tanadar of Bezwara, to the chief Masulipatam.

I have, by your Honours favour, cultivated the countries, through the means of both the old and new inhabitants, having sown Janaloo seeds on some fields, and others still remain unsowed for want of rain, which shall get them done, as soon as the rain sets, in the supplyment with necessaries to the garrison of Condapilly, puts still the people of this district in great inconveniences; some troops and some officers are now encamped at this place, drive the Bramnies, &c. from their habitations, taken their houses for their reception, and for that purpose is in great confusion. The inhabitants also suffer much inconveniency for supplying them daily with Coolies for their chests and sundries; if a continuance of such trouble is not removed, at this time, being most proper for cultivation, and this Paraganah is rather too small, to bear such troubles, how can I keep it in good order? I am uncertain how long the army will continue here; but during their stay, you will order necessary to be supplied them, both from this and other countries; for the inhabitants can

no

‡ The latter end of December 1778, the Tanadar of Bezwara declared under his hand, in the presence of several people, that he never made any complaints, nor had any cause to complain to the chief and council, of the behaviour of the detachment at Bezwara. See his deposition, and the letters from lieutenant Russel and Forbes, pages 68, 69, 70.

no longer endure the trouble of supplying them: if otherwise, land custom of this Paraganah is settled by the company to the amount of 400, and afterwards 200 increased more, and in all 600 pagodas, which · amount the company receives yearly. But these people now here raised a Bazar, fixed Choukeedars in different places, and receives the customs for themselves, and putting a stop from collecting us the usual custom of this Paraganah. As I am your servant, I write these affairs to inform your Honour with.

I hope you will be pleased to order to the abovesaid land customs business, and for supplying necessaries how you think proper.

Small grain of Mylavaram district is ready to cut, therefore I write this to acquaint you with.

A true Copy. *Thomas Barnard*, Secretary.

Major Mathews, to Anthony Sadleir, Esq; chief and council of Masulipatam.

Gentlemen,

I have the pleasure of acquainting you, that I shall be near Bezwara to-morrow morning.

Since my addressing you concerning the rumour of the French ship being off Mutapilly, a detachment from captain Barclay's battalion, under the command of lieutenant Grant is stationed at Baumpetla.

A detachment of sepoys, with one gun, under the command of lieutenant Brown, are at Coringy, for the security of that port.

Captain Lane has informed me, that he had ordered lieutenant Nelson, with a company of sepoys, to join Peryrauze, to assist him in securing the Peddapore district from the ravages of Rajanahdourah. And that those people belonging to the Vizagapatam district,

strict, that Venkatyrauze had sent to join Peryrauze, were gone back to Gulgundah. Captain Lane also mentioned that Rajanah-dourah had sent agents to him, with offers to cease his depredations, in case he should be allowed to have the management of part of the Tontapilly country. To which I put captain Lane in mind of what he had heretofore been told of; that it was your directions Rajanah-dourah should be allowed no other terms than *unconditional submission*.

I must request of you to comply with the last indents that I sent to you from Ellore and Bezwara.

I have the honour, &c.

Richard Mathews.

Chicacolum, Dec. 8, 1778.

Major Mathews, to Anthony Sadlier, Esq; chief and council of Masulipatam.

Gentlemen,

Your letter of the 19th of November, covering a complaint of the Tanadar of Bezwara, I received in due time.

Herewith you will have extracts of letters from the officers, who have commanded the detachment at Bezwara, in reply to the Tanadar's complaint. So far as it relates to myself, you were informed of shortly after that the troops were, by my directions, stationed there. I have lately been at Bezwara, with an intention of desiring the Tanadar to make known the people who had committed abuses, as you are pleased to call the tenor of his letter, and I think without reason; but he was not to be found, having left that place a few days before my arrival. Upon enquiry I could not discover any abuses, which makes me suppose that his absence has not been occasioned by the troops now there. The owners of four or five houses, which are all that are occupied by officers or others, the

sepoys

sepoys being lodged in public buildings, may have great reason to be dissatisfied, but no others. Therefore I fancy that *Calabarga Juggiah's letter is " of a piece" with Ragojee's petition.

The chief and council of Masulipatam, for many years, have not been ignorant in what manner the honourable company's orders,† under date the 23d of March 1770, have been in force in this district. Should the honourable select committee, or the chief and council think proper to make a new regulation that will be of advantage to the service, I shall most readily concur; being more inclined to exert myself for the benefit of the company, than to expose myself to the vindictive spirit of my enemies, by disobeying the orders of my employers, and the articles of war.

On the 3d of November, I requested of you to order Ragojee to furnish proofs of his assertions, and let me know the names of his evidences. As I suppose that the petition *may have been sent to Madras*, because you say in your letter of the 29th ult. in answer to mine of the 3d ult. that you " shall transmit" a copy of my reply to Ragojee's complaint, " to the honourable select committee;" and truly, considering how far it affected the future welfare of the injured inhabitants, it should have been transmitted to the honourable the select committee on the 6th ult. you having received it on the 4th. Thirty-six days have now elapsed, and I cannot perceive any sign of your doing me justice. Therefore, I again call upon you for the evidences, that I may apply to the commander in chief to prevent in future such unworthy reflections upon the commanding officer of the troops in this district, as you have hitherto thrown upon me; and thereby wounding in me, every officer in the service, who in future may succeed to so honourable a station.

An

---

* See Note, and the Tanadar's deposition, page 68.

† That Bazar duties should not be levied by the commanding officer.

An exract of a letter from captain Lane, dated 6th inftant, will inform you what has been done by the honourable company's tributaries with Rajanah-dourah. The officer has repeatedly had my orders conformable to your fentiments of "unconditional fubmiffion." But inftead of fubmiffion to, or future dependence of any kind upon, the honourable company, he, and thofe concerned, have treated, as far as comes to my knowledge, totally independent of them. And him whom you reprefent as "a rebel and a murderer," owes his prefent peace to conditions that reflect upon the juftice of the company. In this I fhall no ways interfere without your further directions.

Some people of mine, that have been at Neirmull, fay, that Fauzel beg Chan had at that place about one thoufand horfe and five thoufand fepoys, and was raifing more fepoys. Not any rupture with the Soubah talked of, nor do I think it likely, their general intereft being fo much at ftake, by the march of the troops from Bengal towards Poonah, and the treaties that our war with France may occafion. It would be folly for the Soubah and his General to fall out, when they might gain more by joining, for, or againft us. It has been repeatedly faid, that Fauzel beg Chan had an eye to the poffeffion of our Circars; I may fafely fay, that he has a foot in them; for he is upon the beft terms with the Rajah of the *Cicacole diftrict, whofe Vakeel is now with him in all the pomp of the Eaft, whilft the company's Vakeel, at the fame place, has only the appearof a common Dubafh.†

Niermull is about eight days journey to the weftward of Rajamundry. On the road, about fixty miles from Rajamundry, is a town and a fmall diftrict, called Paulunfey Burdachalem, that three

or

---

* Sitteramrauze and his family.

† This is the perfon of truft, mentioned in a letter from the chief and council, of no date, but received the 13th of September.

or four years ago Fauzel beg Chan gave to Sittaramrauze, as a Jaghire for his son, now an infant. By this place the communication is kept up from Neirmull to our Circars.

A man from Chinterpilly says, that in Waſſyreddy-ramanah's camp it is reported, that they expect a large body of horse to join them from Niermull. It is possible that there may not be any foundation for such report; however, considering every circumstance of the present time, it will help to put us on our guard. I shall send officers to take a view of the different passes leading from the westward to this district; also, of the forts on our frontiers, that in case the Circars should be threatened, every place of defence may be known.

I must again request that you will be pleased to supply the troops at Ellore and Bezwara with the stores indented for the 17th of October.

As I was on the point of concluding, the accompanying letter came in from lieutenant Russell. I have ordered him to prepare for marching. And, my being so near Masulipatam as four miles, I may hope, from you, an immediate answer, expressive of your sentiments upon the subject. You are already in possession of mine, by my letters of the 20th, 22d and 26th of October.

I have the honour, &c.

Richard Mathews.

Gundoor, Dec. 13, 1778.

Major Mathews, to Anthony Sadleir, Esq; chief and council of Masulipatam.

Gentlemen,

I wrote to you the day before yesterday, concluding the letter with very material intelligence, which I had that instant received from lieutenant

lieutenant Ruſſel. You were, upon three different times, in the month of October, acquainted with my ſentiments concerning the ſtep that Chelacauney Juggiah and Venkiah of Newjure had taken; alſo, had before you a copy of my orders to enſign Wilſon, which muſt impreſs you with an opinion, that upon the ſame occaſion I would act in a ſimilar manner, the circumſtances being now the ſame, but ſomewhat nearer the point of execution by the actual march of the Peons towards the Kiſtna.

I had every reaſon to ſuppoſe that ere this time you would have favoured me with your directions, which, if forwarded in due time, might have been delivered to me in three hours after your receiving my letter. In one of your letters to me, dated in October, you ſay, that the meaſure I took, in ſending enſign Wilſon to Newjure, was unwarrantable, and might have occaſioned hoſtilities. My diſtant ſituation from you, at that time, induced me to iſſue orders that would be effectual, without waiting for your advice. But as I am now, and was when I wrote to you on the 13th, within five miles of Maſulipatam, I have, as far as the nature of the ſervice would admit, attended for your ſentiments on the matter, as to the ultimate mode of execution, which, your delay in giving, may be productive of bad conſequences.

The papers accompanying this will ſhew you what has been done. Mr. Ruſſel had orders from me to uſe every means in his power, except attacking them, to prevent the troops belonging to Chelacauney Venkiah croſſing the river, or paſſing to the weſtward of Condapilly. But as theſe orders, for want of power to employ force, may be ineffectual, you will be pleaſed to inform me, with all convenient ſpeed, to what lengths I muſt go to oblige our tributary Chelacauney Venkiah, not to ſend troops to attack our tributary Waſſyreddy-ramanah in the country belonging to Bafalat Jung, and to compel him, Venkiah, to diſband thoſe aſſembled; alſo to give

ſecurity

security for his not raising an armed force in the honourable company's district, which in itself is a measure that must carry with it a greater idea of independence than the safety of the company's property will admit.

I purpose going this afternoon to Chicolum,* where I should be glad to hear from you.

By a part of lieutenant Russel's letter, you will perceive the small quantity of fuzee ammunition that is with his party. I must once more request that my indents be complied with as soon as possible.

The select picquet of the 7th battalion, that some time ago I had (on account of discipline) sent to Condapilly, I have ordered to join lieutenant Russel.

I have the honour to be, &c.
Richard Mathews.

Gundoor, Dec. 15, 1778.

Major Mathews, to Anthony Sadleir, Esq; chief and council of Masulipatam.

Gentlemen,

I inclose a paper of intelligence that I received this morning. Mr. Forbes is at Madoor; I have not heard any thing material from him, excepting that Chelacauney Venkiah promised to discharge the Peons that were assembled, and to go himself to Newjure. This was on the 15th in the morning; but the same evening, my Hircar says, that four hundred Peons came to Madoor. In a letter of this morning at one o'clock, Mr. Forbes says, that Venkiah is to set off this morning for Newjure. A few hours will discover whether he really goes to Newjure, and disperses his Peons, or not.

Letters by the Bezwara Tappal will come safe.

I have the honour, &c.
Richard Mathews.

Chicacolum, Dec. 16, 1778.

---

* Five miles from the place where Chelacauney Venkiah had assembled his troops, and close to the river Kistna.

The Chief and Council of Mafulipatam, to Major Mathews.

Sir,

We have received your letters under date the 5th and 13th inftant. We highly difapprove of the conduct of *Chelacauney Juggiah, the manager in Operrow's country; and if it be found to correfpond entirely, with the account lieutenant Ruffell has given of it, and it appears that he has actually embodied troops, let it be for any purpofe whatever, for, without the fanction of government, fuch an act muft, in any cafe, be criminal, we are of opinion he ought to be feized and fent to this place, that proper meafures may be taken with him, to deter others from the like conduct in future. We do therefore require of you, to take the neceffary fteps for this purpofe: and we think that the appearance of any confiderable number of armed men, collected together in any part of the country, under the fuperintendance of the above Chelacauney Juggiah, who cannot give a fatisfactory account of themfelves, will be a fufficient ground to warrant, and fully juftify, the officer you may pleafe to fend on this fervice, in proceeding to execute what we have required. We fend you copy of the reply of the above manager, to the letter addreffed to him by our chief, in confequence of fome proceedings of a fimilar nature, with which you formerly acquainted us, as the contents may poffibly be of fome ufe. You will pleafe to recommend to the officer to be employed on this occafion, that his prifoner be treated with all the attention he can poffibly fhew him, without endangering an efcape.

We now proceed to the further fubject of your above letters. The whole bufinefs of Rajanah-dourah has been long before the honourable felect committee. Copies of all that you have communicated will also be tranfmitted to them; and a proper attention will, no doubt, be

---

* They miftook the man. The perfon in arms was Chelacauney Venkiah.

be paid in the end, not only to your remarks and reflections, but to the subject in general. We must therefore, in this particular, wait a communication from our superiors, of which, as far as you are concerned, you will be duly acquainted.

We must now touch on a subject, which, if your charge were justly founded, would affect us with the most unfeigned concern; it has never been our intention, Sir, to cast unworthy reflections upon any one; nor are we conscious of having thrown any upon you: every part of our correspondence with you, to which this charge can refer, is already before the honourable select committee; to their justice we make our appeal: and shall earnestly entreat of them that they will not fail to inflict the punishment, whenever it may appear due. We hope, Sir, that, in the issue of this trial, it will sufficiently appear, that the gentlemen of the army, whom you very unnecessarily, unless it were with a view to stir up a spirit of party, have associated in your cause, and represent to be wounded, through the treatment you have received, cannot, by any part of our conduct, have sustained the least hurt: nor do we believe, Sir, it has ever been impeached by them. We now proceed to reply more particularly to those passages in your letter we have just been remarking upon. Ragojee's petition was transmitted to the presidency, as you suppose. We were under a necessity of communicating your charge against him; justice then required we should make no distinction between you, but communicate equally for both, whatever might be offered. This being the case, we do not see what pretence there is for arraigning our conduct. It has been passive, with respect to you, in every instance, where you have not compelled us into action; and we think it not altogether unworthy of remark, that in the matter from which your present complaints spring, you were yourself the original; and, as we conceive, (it being out of your line, at least to do it in the manner you did) the officious mover therein: but, whether it be so or not, we have submitted it to our superiors. Respecting the complaints

plaints at Bezwara, we beg your attention to what was written you upon that subject: we believe, that what we have said upon that occasion, cannot, by any, the most forced construction, be interpreted into the language of accusers; it was, perhaps, blameable in the contrary extreme. We observed to you, that the complaint was of an early date; of course, that it had not been much attended to, although it had even been often repeated. And, lastly, we only desire of you, to take such measures as the result of the enquiry might point out to be necessary, without asking any account of your proceedings therein. We were sensible that complaints of this kind are often made without just cause: and it was this persuasion that induced us to overlook a former complaint on the same subject, which we did not transmit to you, as well as to neglect so long the one we did. But, after all, we cannot perceive that the Tanadar is so much mistaken in what he has asserted: the injury to some of the inhabitants, by taking possession of their houses, is acknowledged. The establishment of a Bazar is equally so; and we believe that it will not be controverted, that wherever five or six hundred sepoys, and any number of Europeans, however small, come to fix themselves in a station, the neighbouring country will be distressed in the article of coolies, for the necessary business of the cantonments; throwing up mud walls to houses or huts, and numberless little services that we may be unable to specify. We do not mention the permission of this, as a crime in the commanding officer; for we do not think it can often, without distress to the troops, especially going into monsoon quarters, be prevented; but we mention it, as giving a colour of probability to the Tanadar's complaint.* Respecting the Bazar, the officer commanding at Bezwara should have applied to the country government to be provided with one; and not have established one dependent on himself: whatever precautions may be taken, it is

not

---

* The chief and council take great pains to render the complaint *probable*; but see the Tanadar's deposition, note page 68.

not poſſible, but that ſuch a meaſure muſt be injurious to the revenue of the diſtrict where it happens; and perhaps more ſo, where, as at Bezwara, the amount of the cuſtoms is inconſiderable, amounting only to pagodas 600 per year. We ſhall here conclude this ſubject, and, if what we have ſaid reſpecting it, ſhould appear deficient in any reſpect, by being tranſmitted to the honourable ſelect committee, as we mean to do with the whole of this letter, an opportunity will thereby be given of having it amended.

We do not think it expedient juſt now to ſend the ſtores you have indented for, to Ellore and Bezwara. We daily expect orders from the preſidency, in conſequence of which, a new arrangement of the troops may take place; and as theſe ſtores cannot be wanted for any ſervice immediately going forward, by ſending them at this time to the above places, we ſhall only incur a uſeleſs expence; in carrying them to ſtations, which, the troops may, even almoſt before the ſtores can arrive at them, be ordered to quit.

We are, &c.

Anth. Sadleir,
James Hodges,
Thomas Barnard.

Maſulipatam, Dec. 15, 1778.

P. S. We have juſt now received your letter of this day's date; the particular ammunition therein mentioned ſhall be forwarded without delay.

Major Mathews, to Anthony Sadleir, Eſq; chief and council of Maſulipatam.

Gentlemen,

I have received your letter of the 15th inſtant. My letters of the 13th and 15th will ſhew you, that Chelacauney Venkiah (not Juggiah)

giah) was the man who, it was reported, was assembling people with an intention of crossing the river to join Monickrow. As I supposed that you by mistake mentioned Juggiah, who did not stir from, and is now at, Newjure, instead of Venkiah, I did not issue orders for the march of a party to seize the man whose name was not used as the offending person; but put the spirit of your requisition into execution upon the person of Chelacauncy Venkiah, who will be delivered to you by Lieutenant Forbes.

Of your letter of the 15th, those parts that concern myself are not at this time deserving of any notice; upon comparing this your production with the others of the same spirit that I have been favoured with, my assertions will evidently appear to all unprejudiced men to be founded in fact, and as such I shall at all times be ready to answer.

I have the honour to be, &c.

Richard Mathews.

Chicacolum, Dec. 18, 1778.

Major Mathews, to Edward Cotsford, Esq; chief and council of Masulipatam.

Gentlemen,

The orders of the 22d ult. having deprived me of that command which appeared to me necessary for the good of the service, and which was conformable to the orders of the honourable the court of Directors; I beg leave to acquaint you, that I shall decline acting, more especially as at this time I have not any troops immediately under my command, and my former authority, over those not present, ceasing.

I have this day acquainted the commander in chief of my intent, and have applied for permission to go to Madras.

I have the honour, &c.

Richard Mathews.

Masulipatam, Jan. 2, 1779.

Not

Not any answer to the above, or to my letter of the same date to General Munro, and of the 3d to Sir Eyre Coote. The following was the mode observed by the select committee, &c.

Mr. Pringle, to Major Mathews.

Sir,

I am directed by the chief and council to acquaint you, that the honourable select committee, in consequence of your having applied through the commander in chief for leave of absence to proceed to the presidency, have granted you leave of absence accordingly.

I am, sir, &c.

Alexander Pringle, Secretary.

Masulipatam, *Jan.* 19, 1779.

APPENDIX.

Extracts of Letters from Major Mathews, *to Officers commanding Detachments in the Circars, dependent upon* Mafulipatam.

Major Mathews, to lieutenant Thomas Meek, commanding at Ventapollam.

Sir,

THE Ongole companies, and three companies from Mafulipatam, I have ordered to take poſt at Sandole: if you are the ſenior officer, you are to take upon you the command of them, and retire with your company to join them.

We are at peace with Bafalat Jung; ſo you will not give him cauſe to be offended; but you are to do your utmoſt to prevent any injury to the company's country.

As far as poſſible you are to act on the defenſive, and at all events ſecure your retreat to Nauggalanka, on the ſouthern bank of the Kiſtna. Should you hear of the approach of Lally's party towards the Guntoor Circar, you will inſtantly retreat to the place above-mentioned, and avoid an action, except you can command it on the moſt advantageous terms. Should you be certain that Lally's force moves towards Ongole, with a ſeeming intention of attacking it, you are to remain at or near Sandole; but go no farther ſouth without orders.

Richard Mathews.

Cicacole, Aug. 22, 1778.

Major Mathews, to Lieutenant Doveton.

Sir,

You received orders from captain Johnſtone to join captain Bridges at Condapilly; but there hath ariſen a neceſſity of altering your route. Upon receipt of this you will march to this place, then croſs the Kiſtna, and proceed to Sandole: upon your arrival there you will give lieutenant Meek, who is at Ventapollam, notice of your ſituation, and obſerve his directions. Two companies from Ongole are to join you; I do not know the rank of the officer who commands them; but the ſenior officer is to take command of the five companies, when joined.

You will leave at Cicacole one Jemadar, one Havaldar, two Naikes, and eighteen ſepoys, in charge of the four boats that were ſent from Maſulipatam: they are not to be removed from hence without my orders.

You muſt ſupply yourſelf with rice for your party; I do not believe you can procure any at this place.

I ſhall go from hence to Condapilly; in four or five days return to this place, and then go down the river to Yendarah, the part where the Tappy croſſes to Nauggalanka; where in future I believe the boats will be ſtationed.

You will be pleaſed to give me frequent advice of your ſituation, and of all occurrences: take the utmoſt care to prevent any injury

to

to the inhabitants, either of our country or the Guntoor Circar: in respect to the latter, you will be cautious of giving offence.

Lieutenant Meek informed me, that a Frenchman, at the head of five hundred sepoys, and some small guns, was at Pottarum, ten cofs from Ventapollam. This will be sufficient to put you on your guard.

Richard Mathews.

Cicacole, *on the banks of the Kistna*, Aug. 22, 1778.

Major Mathews, to captain Thomas Bridges.

Sir,

With the detachment under your command, you will do your utmost to protect that part of the Circars belonging to the honourable company, which is south of the Kistna; and to be attentive to the motions of a party under Mr. Lally, reputed to be in the service of Basalat Jung; or to any troops that may be forming in the Guntoor Circar.

You will demand of lieutenant Meek copies of my orders to him, and as far as possible conform thereto; with this latitude, that I do not confine your movements to the southward only to Sandole, but to the extent of the company's country.

You will be cautious to secure a timely retreat to Nauggalanka, or take a good post, according to the intelligence that you may have of the strength of the enemy.

You will acquaint the honourable select committee of any motions of the enemy that seem to threaten an invasion of the Nabob's or our country; and you will at all times communicate to me every material occurrence, so that I may be certain of your situation.

By keeping up a correspondence with the officer commanding at Ongole, you may be better enabled te fullfil the intent of your expedition.

Richard Mathews.

Condapilly, Aug. 24, 1778.

Major Mathews, to the officer commanding a detachment from captain Powell's battalion at Yanam.

Sir,

Upon receipt hereof you will march with your detachment to Samulcotah, and from thence attend the motions of Rajanah-dourah of Tontapilly, who (it is reported to me) is preparing to invade our districts, or the country belonging to our tributaries.

You will do your utmost to protect all those dependent upon the company, and demand assistance from the people belonging to Peddapore, or Pettapore, or any of the Zemindaries whose lands are threatened with invasion. Should they fail in giving the necessary assistance, which is so much for their own security, you will acquaint me therewith, and not fail to give me constant and early information of every occurrence; and to observe my orders agreeably to the honourable company's regulations of military service there laid down for subordinacies.

You are not to consider the fortress of Samulcotah as a defence, but you are to meet the invaders (in whatever part may be threatened) for the security of the country. But you are not to go among the hills, which hath already been the grave of so many of our countrymen.

Richard Mathews.

Camp at Condeer, Aug. 26, 1778.

Major

Major Mathews, to captain Thomas Bridges.

Sir,

Serjeant Palmer writes, that the abfent fepoys do not return, and particularly, that the Tanadar of Newjure would not let the fepoys join their battalion.

Sept. 3, 1778.

Richard Mathews.

Major Mathews, to captain Thomas Bridges.

Sir,

I fuppofe that you will have people at Condavier to watch the motions of Rajah Rahader, and of the French; particularly if there is the leaft indication of an intended movement to the fouthward.

Sept. 4, 1778.

Richard Mathews.

Major Mathews, to captain Barclay, at Ongole.

Sir,

I have not heard any thing particular of Bafalat Jung, or Lally; but I fuppofe from circumftances that the firft motions will be towards you. Captain Bridges will be on the look out.

Sept. 4, 1778.

Richard Mathews.

Major Mathews, to captain George Nixon, at Rajamundry.

Sir,

The accompanying lift will introduce to you the Jemadars, Havaldars, Naikes, and fepoys ordered to you from the fecond battalion. You are to obferve, that they are to be confidered according to the list as Jemadars, Havaldars, Naikes, and sepoys, and not to be promoted till further orders; and you will acquaint them that their promotion will depend upon their zeal and activity in assisting you to form your battalion.

Richard Mathews.

Sept. 7, 1778.

Major Mathews, to lieutenant Moslay, commanding a detachment south of the Kistna.

I am sorry to hear that the inhabitants of some villages belonging to Basalat Jung have run away from their houses.

You will do your utmost to assure them, that we have not any hostile intention towards Basalat Jung, and that you will protect them equally with the company's people.

Richard Mathews.

Sept. 10, 1778.

Major Mathews, to captain James Powell.

Sir,

You will proceed with your battalion to Sandole, and take upon you the command of the troops of this Circar, that are now under the orders of captain Bridges, at or near Baumpetlah. The force you are to detain, is to depend upon the intelligence that captain Bridges or you may have, on the 15th of this month, of the situation of Mr. Lally's party, and of the troops assembling in the Guntoor Circar.

My last accounts say, that he (Mr. Lally) was at Adoni, the 29th ultimo; and although there were at that time no extraordinary preparations for marching, yet he was encamped, had every thing necessary for moving, and it was said, that after the 15th of this month, at the conclusion of the Desarey feast, he was to come with his own troops,

troops, and the cavalry belonging to Bafalat Jung, towards Guntoor.

Should you have no account of his approach on the 15th, you are to order captain Bridges, with what number of his battalion you think proper, to join me by the way of Nuggalanka, where the company's boats are. You will demand a fight of the orders that I gave to lieutenant Meek, and to captain Bridges, making them, as far as poffible, your guide. Your views will be,

Firſt. The protection of the company's country.

Secondly. To hang upon Monſieur Lally's rear, ſhould he attempt to go to the ſouthward, by the way of Ongole; and in ſuch a caſe, by every means in your power, to impede his march.

Thirdly. To prevent the landing of men or military ſtores to reinforce Mr. Lally.

Fourthly. To prevent Monſieur Lally's embarking any part of his force.

Fifthly. To act offenſively againſt any party headed by a Frenchman, that ſhould have a hoſtile appearance towards us.

You are to obſerve, that although we are on friendly terms with Bafalat Jung, you are not to put too much faith upon his amicable profeſſions. His detaining ſuch a number of our enemies in his ſervice, is ſufficient to put us upon our guard. At the ſame time, you are not to enter haſtily the country belonging to Bafalat Jung, excepting to execute, in the moſt prudent and determined manner, any part of your orders.

You are, from time to time, to give the honourable ſelect committee conſtant information of every intelligence worthy their knowledge, ſending to them a copy of this letter; and if they are pleaſed to diſapprove of any part of it, you will obey their orders, giving me advice thereof; and, at all times, make me acquainted with every occurrence.

You will correspond with the officer commanding at Ongole, and be in readiness to assist him, should he be attacked.

Richard Mathews.

Sept. 10, 1778.

Major Mathews, to lieutenant Archibald Brown, commanding a detachment near Samulcotah.

Sir,

I would have you provide good bullocks for the guns, with bad you will not be able to move so expeditiously as may be necessary.

Should not the Peddapore, or other countries, eastward of the hills, be threatened by Rajah-dourah, and that he has broke up from before Routlapunda, you will march your detachment in the fort of Samulcotah, and place them in the barracks; but they are to have every thing necessary for moving at the shortest notice.

Richard Mathews.

Sept. 25, 1778.

Major Mathews, ro captain Thomas Bridges.

Sir,

The chief and council of Masulipatam having represented to me, that they require a reinforcement to the present garrison of Masulipatam, and as I cannot meet their wishes in a better manner than by furnishing you with authority to be a security to the fort of Masulipatam, I desire that you will, upon receipt hereof, repair to Masulipatam, and, advising the chief and council therewith, take upon you the charge of the fort and garrison of Masulipatam, agreeably to the rules of service, and the honourable company's regulations. At

the

the same time I inclose to you a copy of a paragraph of a letter, said to be received from the honourable select committee, dated the 19th Sept. 1778, relative to the order that I gave out, concerning sepoys employed on pretence of revenue service.

" We also much difapprove of the order being issued in your garrison, without your consent, and direct, that in future, no garrison order whatsoever be published until it has received your sanction."

Richard Mathews.

Sept. 26, 1778.

Major Mathews, to lieutenant Archibald-Brown.

Sir,

At this unhealthy season, I would have you confine your operations to the security of the country eastward of the hills, and not go among them, excepting, if, by a sudden incursion of one day, or two at most, an advantage might be gained over the enemy, by beating up their quarters.

Richard Mathews.

Sept. 29, 1778.

Major Mathews, to captain Thomas Bridges, at Masulipatam.

Sir,

I have received your letter of the 28th. It was my intention that, agreeably to the orders of the honourable select committee, copy of which I sent you, that you should apply to the chief and council for their sanction, to take upon you the command of the troops in the garrison.

I suppose that they will inform me why they object to your exercising the authority I intended you should have, according to the rules of the service.

Richard Mathews.

Sept. 29, 1778.

Major Mathews, to Captain Thomas Lane, commanding the first Circar battalion, at Samulcotah.

Sir,

When you was at Ellore, I did myself the pleasure of informing you of the general and particular orders that I had given to lieutenant Brown, of which he will acquaint you. This day I received a letter from him, dated the 29th ultimo, advising me of his intention to march as the next day; in order to restore peace to the country of the Rajah Timrauze, by expelling Rajanah-dourah and his people therefrom. It is not my wish, that, at this unhealthy season, the troops should go among the hills, excepting they can effect something very material, and return in two days. We must wait for a more favourable season to expel Rajanah-dourah and his followers from the Tontapilly country. In the mean time, our attention must be to protect the Peddapore and Pettapore countries. The latter, it is thought, assists the enemy, of which you will endeavour to obtain certain information, that punishment may follow such a breach of duty.

Should there be a necessity of having any of your people near the hills, you will find Darmarum to be a good situation, for the protection of the countries east of the hills. It is ten cofs from Samulcotah, four cofs from Tontapilly, in the mouth of that valley; and two or three cofs from Bendapundy, which is in the entrance of Rontlapunda valley. It is high ground, and there is plenty of good water. You will, in a few days, be able to judge what number are necessary

sary to be stationed at that place, or at any other, and recall all that you can to Samulcotah, that you may be enabled to bring your people to some order by the month of January, when we have every reason to expect urgent occasions for all the men we can muster.

You are to pay attention to the security of the company's country, in general, that is near you, and, in particular, to the port of Coringy.

October 1, 1778.
              Richard Mathews.

Major Mathews, to captain Thomas Bridges, commanding the troops at Masulipatam.

My letter to you of the 29th, will shew that I wish to act in conformity to the orders of the honourable select committee, who have directed, that no *garrison order whatsoever* shall be issued in the fort of Masulipatam, without the sanction of the *chief and council*; but I believe that such may be a mistake, for by it the accustomary authority that the chief hath hitherto exercised, seems to be annulled. I do not mention this to induce you to interfere with the prerogative of the chief, for I shall be happy to have the civil and military on such terms, that the service of the company may be properly conducted.

October 2, 1778.
              Richard Mathews.

Major Mathews, to lieutenant N. S. W. Abbott, commanding at Ventapollam.

I have heard that Mr. Whitehill has some concerns with Monsieur Riviere, and that the latter owes the former some money; this may be the cause of the liberty granted to the Frenchmen. I desire you to enquire into this circumstance: and be particular in noticing every

every thing that they do, for no doubt but they will correspond with Monsieur Lally, who commands the troops with Basalat Jung.

Richard Mathews.

October 4, 1778.

Major Mathews, to captain Lane.

Sir,

I have received your letter of the 7th, advising me that you purposed marching to Wafercotah, and that Peryrauze would wish that you should remain some days at Wafercotah.

You are not to let any consideration induce you to act against the orders that I have given you, "not to remain among the hills;" for at this time the preservation of the men, and bringing them to order, are very material objects, which you may attend to, and at the same time secure the open country.

If Timrauze's people are so cowardly as to be incapable of securing the Tontapilly country, they should not be suffered to interfere with it; for, on the present plan, the whole loss falls upon the company's troops, that are already too few for the protection of the Circars.

Richard Mathews.

Oct. 10, 1778.

Major Mathews, to Lieutenant N. S. W. Abbot.

Sir,

You must have spies on the conduct of the Frenchmen; if they correspond with Lally or others concerning our military or political operations, they should be checked: but being allowed to trade, they must correspond on that head with whom they please. Should they act inconsistent with their parole, Basalat Jung's territory is not

to

to be a security to them, any more than it was at the time they were seized by order of the select committee.

Richard Mathews.

October 11, 1778.

Major Mathews, to captain Lane.

Sir,

I request that you will enquire of Peryrauze, or any of Timrauze's managers, at what time Rajanah-dourah began to collect people with a view of entering the Tontapilly country, and the time he did enter it; also, from whom he received assistance; for, of himself, he was not able to keep together a fortnight the number of people he assembled. Captain Powel left Samulcotah about the 20th of August, at which time it appears that the country was only alarmed; and the very next intelligence was, that Routlapunda was attacked. Make yourself master of this subject.

Richard Mathews.

October 12, 1778.

Major Mathews, to captain Lane.

Sir,

I congratulate you upon your success in the first essay among the hills; a small detachment properly conducted will answer almost every purpose. I have not any reason to alter my former orders. The preservation of the open country and of your people are to be your principal objects.

The chief and council of Masulipatam say, that the rule of my conduct towards Rajanah-dourah is to bring him to *unconditional submission*. In my opinion it is impossible to do so; the nature of the country, climate and inhabitants are for him, and the natives, I am told,

told, are much averse to Timrauze: so that our task will be full of difficulties and not to be effected for some time (probably years); but such are the politics of the seat of revenue, and which we must observe.

Richard Mathews.

October 16, 1778.

Major Mathews, to Ensign Wilson.

Sir,

Having heard that Juggiah and Venkiah, managers for the Zemindar Nerriah, have been desired by Monickrow, a tributary to Basalat Jung, to assist him with troops against another Zemindar of the Guntoor Circar; and that Juggiah and Venkiah have agreed, and do intend to send four or five hundred men from Newjure, and as many from Wicure and Madore, across the Kistna, to join Monickrow. As their so doing may at this time involve the company's affairs in some difficulties, you are to prevent it. You are to deliver the accompanying letter, and to acquaint them that you have positive orders to force them to dismiss their levies; and that in future they are not to presume to raise any number of armed men, upon any pretence whatever, without authority from the chief and council of Masulipatam.

You will instantly take measures to oblige them to disband their troops; and when you are certain that they have done so, you are to return to Ellore.

Juggiah and Venkiah are to be informed, that if, after having this notice, they persist in raising men, they shall be considered as enemies, and be punished accordingly.

Should the above-mentioned men act contrary to the orders you will deliver to them, and determine to send troops to assist Monickrow,

nickrow, you are to send advice thereof to the officer commanding at Bezwara, as well as to me; and do your utmost to hinder their crossing the Kistna, by taking possession of all the boats. Should they attempt to force their way, you are to consider them as enemies and attack them with vigour, without any consideration of their numbers.

Inclosed is a translation of my letter to Juggiah and Venkiah.

Richard Mathews.

October 20, 1778.

Translation of a letter from Major Mathews, to Juggiah and Venkiah, managers for Nerriah, Zemindar of Newjure, dated October 19, 1778.

I hear that Monickrow, a man who is tributary to Basalat Jung, has applied to you for assistance against a fellow-tributary.

As your Rajah has not any authority to assemble troops in the company's country, you are immediately to desist from collecting any number of men together; and not upon any account, without the orders of the chief and council, presume to think of having an armed force in our Zemindary, or to send a man across the Kistna, to assist Monickrow; which, if you were permitted to do, may involve the company's affairs in some trouble.

I have sent an officer, to oblige you, to discharge those people that you have assembled, and you are, upon receiving this, to do so.

Richard Mathews.

Major Mathews, to Lieutenant Forbes, commanding a detachment at Bezwara.

Sir,

I hear that one of our tributaries is assembling men, under pretence of assisting a Zemindar, belonging to the Guntoor Circar, who

who is at war with Waffyreddy-ramanah; and that 500 men were to march from Newjure, and as many from Wieure and Madore, to crofs the Kiftna, in a day or two. I have fent an officer and fixty men to Newjure, to put a ftop to the levies; and you will, upon receipt hereof, take meafures to prevent any troops crofing the Kiftna, and immediately to fecure all the boats.

Richard Mathews.

October 20, 1778.

Major Mathews, to captain Lane.

Sir,

It is impoffible to permit one of our tributaries to affift another with an armed force to attack a third, and more efpecially without leave.

The junction that you relate appears to me very extraordinary; becaufe I know that Rajanah-dourah hath hitherto been fupported by Viziaramrauze; and that the Vizianergarum family wifh and hath really fought the deftruction of Timrauze's. You will pay particular attention to what is going forward, and forbid the people belonging to Venkatyrauze to enter our diftrict on any pretence.

The company's troops are at all times the propereft to be employed to punifh the difobedient.

Captain Powel hath directions to reinforce you, fhould it be needful.

Richard Mathews.

Nov. 4, 1778.

Major Mathews, to Captain Lane.

Sir,

You are no further to interfere with Rajanah-dourah than to accept of his perfon, by which he will evince *unconditional fubmiffion*, the

the terms that the chief and council are pleased to hold forth. These and the other part of your instructions you will strictly attend to until you receive greater latitude for your movements.

You have not been sufficiently particular concerning the troops that Vankatyrauze sent to assist the managers of Timrauze. As to the purport of their entering the district, which might be known upon their joining Peryrauze, whether the commander made any difficulty in obeying the order to go out of this district, and to what place he has retired: these are points necessary to make clear my correspondence with the chief and council.

You need not move from Samulcotah to take the field, as you mention, excepting that Coringy is threatened by a force superior to lieutenant Brown's detachment, and it seems that lieutenant Nelson's party is strong enough to secure the open country from any material injury that Rajanah-dourah could do it.

Richard Mathews.

Nov. 28, 1778.

Major Mathews, to lieutenant Meek, commanding at Condapilly.

Sir,

I hear that Wassyreddy-ramanah of Chintapilly has sent for, and soon expects, a reinforcement of horse from the Westward. In my letter to you of the 17th ult. I desired you to confine your views of intelligence to the Jemadars between Condapilly and Combamet. Wassyreddy-ramanah has some land on this side of the river, and is security for the Mylavarum man. He should be narrowly watched. I request that you will send men to Chinterpilly, and to his fort on this side of the river, to see what is going forwards.

Richard Mathews.

Dec. 12, 1778.

Major Mathews, to lieutenant James Ruffel, commanding a detachment at Bezwara.

Sir,

I have received your letter of the 12th. You will immediately prepare for marching; and fhould the force you fpeak of attempt to pafs the river, or to go to the weft of Condapilly, you will endeavour to ftop them by every means in your power, excepting actually attacking them.

I fhall order the felect picquet from Condapilly to join you.

Richard Mathews.

Dec. 13, 1778.

Major Mathews, to captain Robert Barclay, commanding at Ongole.

Sir,

Waffyreddy-ramanah has been reinforced by Peons from this diftrict, and has now, it is faid, 8000 Peons, 300 Arabs and Sedees, and 500 horfe. He left Chinterpilly the day before yefterday, and threatens an immediate attack upon a fort belonging to Monickrow. Monickrow expected to be joined by one or two thoufand men from Nerriah's, alias Operrow's country; but I put a ftop to it, by feizing the General, and fending him prifoner to Mafulipatam. Thus affairs hereabouts wear a troublefome appearance.

Richard Mathews.

Dec. 22, 1778.

[19]

The standing Order, issued in they year 1714; explained in March, 1769; and further explained, and declared in its full force and vigour, Nov. 6, 1769.

Whereas the honourable court of directors of the East India company, did, in the year 1714, establish *a standing, irreversible order, never to be broken,* on any occasion, that none of their people should have any dealings with the country governments, in money matters.

And whereas, notwithstanding the said order, many transactions of that kind have, of late years, been suffered to pass, unreproved.

And whereas, the honourable court of directors, in their orders to their president and council of this coast, dated the 17th of May, 1766, speaking of the great sums of money which they understood to have been lent by their servants, and others residing under their jurisdiction, to the Nabob of the Carnatic, at a very high interest, did order and direct, that, from the receipt of the said orders, the receipt of interest to be taken and received, for loans of money, should not exceed 10 per cent. per annum, but did not therein expressly repeat their prohibition of making loans to, or having money transactions with the country governments; whence some doubts have arisen, whether a revocation of the above-recited order, of the year 1714 be not implied, and a permission tacitly given, to make loans, and have other money transactions with the country governments.

That all doubt on this subject may be effectually removed, the president and council do hereby declare, that they do consider the said standing order of the year 1714 as unrevoked, and being in full force and vigour; and, in consequence thereof, they do hereby expressly forbid all servants of the company, civil and military, and all other Europeans residing under their jurisdiction, to *hold any manner*

of

of correspondence, to make loan, or have any money transactions, of what kind soever the same may be; directly, or indirectly, with any of the princes, rulers, or governors of any of the provinces or states in the East Indies; or with any of their ministers or agents, without the especial licence and permission of the president and council, for the time being; except only in such cases as are explained in the resolution of the president and council, in consultation, the 27th of March, 1769: which resolution is in the following words:

It is ordered, That all correspondence and transactions with the country powers, their ministers, or others, intrusted with any department of government or revenue, be reserved, as formerly, to the president only, at the presidency; and to the chiefs of subordinates, touching the affairs of their respective chief-ships; who are to transmit copies of such correspondence to the president: excepting out of this general prohibition, such cases wherein any of the company's servants, charged with any public affairs, requiring such correspondence; and excepting also, all military officers on commands, who are permitted to correspond, touching the necessary affairs of such command; only provided, that in both cases, copies of such correspondence be transmitted, by the first convenient opportunity, to the president and council, or to the chief and council, under whom such servant, civil or military, shall act at the time.

Resolved, that any wilful deviation herefrom, be deemed and construed a breach of orders, and treated as such.

Dated in Fort St. George, the 6th day of November, 1769.

Signed, by order of the president and council,

J. M. Stone, Secretary.

Copy.

A lift of fepoys detached in the Mafulipatam diftrict, in Aug. 1778.

From four companies that garrifoned Condapilly, were detached, to different parts, one hundred and three men.

From two companies that were ftationed at Ellore, were detached thirty-eight men.

From Captain Johnfon's battalion, were detached eighty-two men.

One man had twenty-fix fepoys for his own private bufinefs, who were employed at Innacunda, in the country belonging to Bafalat Jung, and many more were in the fame Circar.

From Captain Powell's eight companies, there were detached one third.

From a company that was ftationed at Yentapollam, all were difperfed but fourteen men, who remained under the command of an enfign.

From three companies of the feventh battalion, which were at Mafulipatam, were detached thirty men.

From Captain Rowles's battalion, were about one hundred and fifty men. Total, about 775 men.

The Chief and Council of Mafulipatam, to Captain James Powell, commanding the troops at Yanam.

Sir,

You will pleafe to deliver over the charge of the property ceded to you by the French, at Yanam, to Mr. William Hamilton, refident of Ingeram; and, it having been determined to withdraw the troops from Samalcotoh, for the prefent, you will pleafe, after leaving a party of one ferjeant, one jemadar, two havaldars, two naigues, and forty fepoys, under the direction of Mr. Hamilton, to march to Ellore,

by

by the way of Samulcotah, leaving at that place one guard of sepoys, to take care of the stores, until they are disposed of by Mr. Westcott, as we shall direct.

We are, &c.

Anthony Sadleir,
James Hodges,
Thomas Barnard.

Masulipatam, Aug. 16, 1778.

P. S. When you arrive at Ellore, you will please to pursue such orders as you may receive from Major Mathews.

Extract of a letter from captain James Powel, to Major Mathews, dated the 15th of August 1778.

I have had a hint from Masulipatam, that I am to join you in camp on the bank of the Kistna. The service to the southward has deprived me of the flower of my battalion. The grenadier companies in these Circars are the only men that we can take any pains with. The battalion companies are so detached on different commands, that we seldom or ever have them together but at the time of the battalions relieving each other. I hear two more batallions are to be raised for this service, great difficulty will be found in effecting it; if you judge a greater force necessary, than is already in these Circars, surely a representation from you would recall the grenadiers of the Masulipatam district, which would be superior to new-raised troops.

Letter from captain James Powel, to Major Mathews, dated August the 17th 1778.

Sir,

I herewith send you a present state of my battalion, accompanied by a return of my camp equipage; by the former you will see how

my

my people are at present scattered, and by the latter the situation my tents are in.

I beg leave to observe to you, that should I be ordered to take the field, I shall stand in need of an entire new set of marquees, and private tents; in all probability, the other battalions that will be employed are in the same want, and Masulipatam will not be able to supply the whole; if the chief and council have no objection, I can here in a short time furnish myself with both.

Since the report of war has prevailed, I have found great difficulty in getting any recruits.

James Powell.

Extract of a letter from captain James Powell, to Major Mathews, dated the 29th of August, 1778.

Rajanah-dourah is the brother of Juggapah-dourah, whom captain Madge was detached against, and whom lieutenant Palk of that detachment killed in a skirmish. Rajanah-dourah was at that time with captain Madge, as an auxiliary against his brother, and succeeded, on his brother's death, to the Zemindary of Tottapilly, or the Shankarum country, which is tributary to Juggypettyrauze, otherwise stiled Timrauze; but he proving equally rebellious as his brother, captain Collins was in November 1776, sent against him, and drove him out of his country: ever since which, detachments have been kept in that district until last January, when it was reported, that the peace of that country was thoroughly established, as Viziaramrauze had given protection to Rajanah-dourah; but since the late revolutions in the Chicacole district, and the absence of Viziarmruze from the Circars, together with the imprisonment of his father, who was by lieutenant M'Gill taken in that country, he threatens once more to enter into it, which caused the alarm I have represented: this man (the father) I have brought with me.

Capt.

Capt. Johnstone, to Major Mathews, commanding the troops in the Circars of the Masulipatam dependency.

Sir,

Pursuant to your orders, I marched out of the garrison of Masulipatam with seven companies of my battalion the 22d instant, at eight o'clock in the morning, having staid all that time to see if I could get any of the stores indented for by you, ready to take with me to camp; but there being no bullocks to be got, I marched out, and left a Jemadars guard to bring them up after me. I returned to the fort myself, in order to hurry them; but there being none ready, I ordered the men to camp, where Mr. Barnard has promised to send the stores as soon as ready; but there are none come yet: whatever is sent I will take particular care of.

Lieutenant Doveton, with the three companies of the 7th Circar battalion, marched this morning at two o'clock, for the banks of the Kistna. I have acquainted the chief and council with your instructions, concerning observing their requisitions, should the enemy appear before Masulipatam. I have also complied with your other orders, with respect to sending off a Havaldar to order in my sepoys upon command, and have given very strict orders to prevent any of my people from injuring the people or any of the inhabitants, and will be careful that the strictest regularity be observed in camp.

Inclosed I beg leave to send you a present state of the seven companies of my battalion now in camp, near Gundoor, and shall be very punctual in informing you for the future of every occurrence that may happen. I write to the chief and council immediately, to inform them of lieutenant Doveton's marching, and none of the stores being yet come to camp, which you indented for.

I am, sir, your's, &c.

James Johnstone.

Camp near Gundoor, Aug. 23, 1778.

The chief and council of Masulipatam, to captain James Powel, commanding the troops at Samulcotah.

Sir,

We have received your letter, under date the 22d instant. Having come to a resolution, for the present, not to issue any orders that may have a tendency to obstruct the arrangements of Major Mathews, we have referred the matter you have communicated to us, to his consideration, that the danger, you have represented with so much reason, may be guarded against; and he will also direct what is to be done with the prisoners.

We are, sir, &c.

Anthony Sadleir,
James Hodges,
Thomas Barnard.

Masulipatam, Aug. 26, 1778.

Capt. Rowles, to Anthony Sadleir, Esq; chief and council of Masulipatam.

Gentlemen,

Having received orders from Major Mathews, to address you on the subject of Lascars, belonging to Masulipatam, which I am directed, in future, to consider as part of the garrison, I am to request that an account of them may be sent me by those whose charge they are now under, specifying the manner they are employed, and the number that can be mustered here in case of an attack.

I am also to advise you, that Major Mathews has directed me to have guns stationed at a proper distance from each other, from hence to Devy-point, for the purpose of repeating signals: that an European and one Lascar be stationed with each gun; and that a serjeant be sent to stay with the guard at Silkindindy, provided with blue lights.

lights, and whatever might be necessary for making night signals, on the approach of any number of ships.

I have inclosed you a return of invalids and pensioners, that Major Mathews has ordered into this garrison.

I am, Gentlemen, your's, &c.

Thomas Rowles.

Masulipatam, Aug. 28, 1778.

Captain Rowles, to Anthony Sadleir, Esq; chief and council of Masulipatam.

Gentlemen,

I cannot help considering this mode of question and answer, by means of the fort Adjutant, as very irregular. If such orders as are sent by me, for your information, should become a subject of deliberation of the chief and council, I request, in future, they may be entered as public record; it is, I mean, to transmit copies of such correspondence to the commander in chief, that I may have his opinion of these matters as a guide for my future conduct.

I am, Gentlemen, your's, &c.

Thomas Rowles.

Masulipatam, Sept. 6, 1778.

A true copy. *Robert Scouler.*

Copy of Queries, sent by Mr. Sadlier, to Mr. Rowles, with the Town Adjutant's remarks.

Masulipatam, Saturday, Sept. 5, 1778.

Query 1. Whether the orders, by Major Mathews, are to be considered as regimental or garrison orders; and, if garrison orders, whether

ther it is meant to shew them to the chief for his approbation, or to be issued independent of him?

Answer, by captain Rowles. Orders by major Mathews cannot be considered regimental. The chief's approbation, or disapprobation of orders, sent by major Mathews, is not to be determined by me, if necessary or not.

Query 2. What instructions captain Rowles received from major Mathews, concerning these orders?

Answer. No other than to insert them in my orderly book.

Queries 3d and 4th. Whether captain Rowles, by " my orderly book," means the garrison orders? Whether he will publish the orders in question, from major Mathews, against the consent of the chief and council? And if Captain Rowles has any doubts, in answering, in the most direct terms, those queries, he may refer them to major Mathews.

Answer. Captain Rowles will consult Major Mathews.

Masulipatam, Sunday, September 6, 1778.

In my presence, captain Rowles's servant delivered to the chief a letter. Captain Rowles had previously informed me, that such letter was, in some measure, an answer to the last queries of yesterday. The chief, on perusing the letter, informed me, that it contained no direct answer to them queries; that, with respect to the orders in question, they remained in the same state as they did yesterday, and that he was ignorant, and should ever consider himself so, of captain Rowles's intention.

I communicated to captain Rowles the chief's sentiments, as fully as far as my memory and conception could furnish me with recollection, and expression adequate thereto; and afterwards asked him, if it was his determination that I should publish major Mathews's orders, now in contest, in the garrison orderly book, without the chief and council's consent; as the chief had, for himself, and for the council, declared, that they were passive, and should continue so, until the 3d and 4th questions of yesterday were satisfactorily answered.

Captain Rowles, in reply to my observations, directed me to publish the orders in question, in the garrison orderly book, and they were issued accordingly.

(Signed)   *S. Towns*, Fort adjutant.

A true copy.   *Robert Scouler*.

Captain Rowles, to Anthony Sadleir, Esq; chief of Masulipatam.

Sir,

I cannot help considering this mode of question and answer, by means of the fort adjutant, as very irregular. If such orders as are sent by me, for your information, should become a subject of deliberation of the chief and council, I request, in future, they may be entered on public record, as I mean to transmit copies of such correspondence to the commander in chief, that I may have his opinion of these matters as a guide for my future conduct.

I am, Sir,

Your most obedient, humble servant,

Thomas Rowles.

Musalipatam, Sept. 6, 1778.

Extract of a letter from captain Rowles, to Major Mathews, dated at Mafulipatam, September 7, 1778.

I hope you will use your utmoſt endeavour to prevent my being hurt in the opinion of the General, or the gentlemen of the board at Madras, by the repreſentation of the board here.

I told Mr. Towns, yeſterday, that as to the order it was relative to the ſepoy corps only, I did not ſee any neceſſity for putting it in the different books in the garriſon : but he refuſed to publiſh the order, unleſs it was entered in the garriſon orderly book.

A true extract.

Robert Scouler.

Captain Rowles, to Major Mathews, commanding the troops in the Circar of Mafulipatam dependency.

Sir,

The incloſed are the queries, with my anſwers, and a letter to the chief, relating to the publication of your orders of the 3d inſtant, which were not publiſhed here till yeſterday. The fort adjutant informed me this morning, that he was directed to deliver them to me, that no improper advantage might be taken of me, as copies were to be tranſmitted to Madras.

I requeſt, Sir, that you will tranſmit a copy of them to the Geneneral, and to the honourable ſelect committee, if you think it neceſſary, that I may not, on the letters from the board here, ſtand cenſured, till matters have been explained by you.

I am, Sir,

Your moſt obedient, humble ſervant,

Thomas Rowles.

Mafulipatam, Sept. 7, 1778.

Captain

Captain Rowles, to Major Mathews.

Dear Sir,

I now send you the copies of the papers I mentioned yesterday. As soon as you have had that which is signed by lieutenant Towns copied, I should be glad if you would return it. "I hope you will use your utmost endeavours to prevent my being hurt in the opinion of the General, or the gentlemen of the board at Madras, by the representation of the board here. I told Mr. Towns, yesterday, that as to the order it was relative to the sepoys corps only; I did not see any necessity for putting it in the different books of the garrison; but he refused to publish the order, unless it was entered in the garrison orderly book."

I am, dear Sir,

With much esteem,

Your most obedient servant,

Thomas Rowles.

Masulipatam, Sept. 7, 1778.

Translation of a letter from Rajah Bahader, of Guntoor, to Major Mathews, Sept. 6, 1778.

I have received your letter, and understand the contents thereof. You wrote to me concerning the sepoys belonging to the company, who are in this country, that, wherever they are, they are to go from thence to join you; so I have wrote, and particularly to Inacundah. There is no manner of difference between company's business and the Nabob's. I look upon that country and this to be the same, now you have wrote to me, and, by your letter, I have encouraged all the
inhabitants

inhabitants not to be afraid of any thing; for the Nabob (Bafalat Jung) and the company are friends. About fome bufinefs I have wrote to the chief of Mafulipatam, of which you will know.

Captain Johnftone, to Major Mathews.

Sir,

As you were pleafed to do me the honour to afk me my opinion, in writing, concerning the quarters allotted for the European commiffioned officers, and the barracks for the fepoys, in the garrifon of Mafulipatam, I beg leave to inclofe you the accompanying lift of them, as they ftood on the 22d of Auguft, on which day I marched out of garrifon to camp.

I am, with great refpect, Sir,

your moft obedient, and humble fervant,

James Johnftone.

Camp at Veyore, Sept. 22, 1778,

Lift of officers quarters, in the garrifon of Mafulipatam, Auguft 22, 1778.

Commanding officer's quarters,	No. 1,	good.
Engineers	No. 2,	ditto. [Room for 2
Captain Rowles's	No. 3,	ditto. fubalterns.]
Artillery officers	No. 4,	ditto.
Fort adjutant's, formerly the battalion adjutant's, but given away by Mr. Davidfon	No. 5,	ditto.
Battalion adjutant's	No. 6,	indifferent.

Dutch Factory, three fubalterns, No. 7, 8, and 9, ready to tumble down.

Other fubalterns quarters, wanting a great deal of repair, No. 10, 11, and 12.

N. B. The

N. B. The quarters that were lieutenant Atwood's and lieutenant Doveton's, are now given away to Mr. Statham and Mr. Keating, and are now no more military quarters. The punch-house, which I got from Mr. Sadleir, for three artillery officers of captain Collins's detachment, is under the charge of Mr. Statham, who has given up a room to lieutenant Anderson, captain Rowles's adjutant, in them; but are not considered as military quarters.

There is one or two other quarters, which is allotted to me for the officers; but such, that none lived in them, but those who could not get better. One of captain Rowles's officers preferred the guard-room, over the Pettah gate.

The only barracks I know, in Masulipatam, for sepoys, were built for a battalion of a thousand strong, (making allowance) for the men on duty, sick, and on command, besides those permitted to sleep out.

There is one battalion store-room belonging to them; and the roof, which is a platform, is supported by one and thirty pillars, round each of which there is room for thirty stand of arms; though I am pretty sure you cannot lodge above six or seven hundred men in them. What other quarters there may be for sepoys, unless you give them the old invalid and pensioners' barracks, I do not know.

There is one pityful house allotted to the commandant of the battalion; the European non-commissioned officers sleep in the places built for guard-rooms, round the fort; and the black commissioned officers, and others, who have leave, or families, in huts, or houses, if they can get them.

These, except the new European barracks, which are not finished, are all the quarters I know of in Masulipatam.

I am, &c. &c.

James Johnstone.

Camp at *Veyere*, Sept. 22, 1778.

Transf-

[33]

Translation of a complaint delivered to Major Mathews, at Ellore, October 8, 1778.

The complaint of Venkahgopunnah, Lingum grumullu, gardener of the charity garden, and the gardener belonging to Veru Vencoyah, who is an inhabitant of Ellore. When we were plowing in the garden, some peons belonging to Ragojee came, and by force took the bullocks from the plough, and carried them away. We said to the peons, that one time before they had taken our bullocks to carry guns to Condapilly, without paying any thing for the use of them, and we were obliged to be at all the travelling expences ourselves, till we returned to Ellore, upon which the peons offered to beat us. Ragojee is receiving pay for his own bullocks, without employing them, and presses ours to do the business. At the time the great guns went to Masulipatam, there was pressed from the inabitants of the Havally 300 bullocks, which were carried as far as Perriquier; then bullocks were pressed from Operrow's country, and ours were released; but we received nothing for their use, or for our own labour and expences.

Of the grain that hath been reaped, we were allowed half the crop, the other half the renter claimed; but he forced us to take his share at the rate of four and a quarter pagodas, per putty; besides, for every putty we were obliged to allow a quarter of a pagoda to Mr. Pringle, and for Operrow's customs, &c. they charged us at the rate of half a pagoda, per putty; which, together, makes the sum of five pagodas per putty, that we are compelled to pay. It is thus that we lose our share of the crop and our money; and till this time they say the balance is against us.

Signed in the original, by Venkinah-gopunnah, Lingum-grumullu, Nanjunah.

Lieutenant

Lieutenant Forbes, to Major Mathews, commanding the troops in the Circars.

Sir,

I have received your letter from Chicacolum. Chelikany Venkia informs me, that his reason for assembling so many peons was, that some peons came from Ongole for two thousand pagodas of Mr. G. which money was lent to Opperrow some months ago; that he had wrote to Masulipatam to Operrow's Duvan, to speak to the chief for permission to raise some peons and cross the river, in order to raise this money, as he has some villages on the other side. He says, the chief, &c. have always allowed him to carry as many peons with him as he chose, when settling the Zemabundey's; but allows that he has not had their permission for this, but expects it daily.

I have ordered him to dismiss his people immediately, and repair to Noongur. He says, he will go to Noongur, whenever I please; but that he must have his people with him, as they all belong to that place, and that he will immediately dismiss them on his arrival there.

I have examined the Ongole peons; they say, they were sent by Mr. G. They have with them nine stand of the company's arms and pouches. They have been from Ongole these fifteen days.

I am, sir, your's, &c.

James Forbes.

Madeer, Dec. 16, 1778.

[35]

Field return of four companies of the second Circar battalion of sepoys, commanded by captain James Powel, cantonments at Ellore, October 19, 1778.

	Captain	Lieutenant	Enfign	Adjutant	Serjeant Major	Quarter-mafter ferjeant	Serjeant	Commandant	Subadar	Jemadar	Havaldar	Naikes	Drummers	Perchalls	Sepoys	Total
Field	1		6	1		1	1	1	5	4	24	20	6		292	352
Duty											2	1		8	21	32
Drill						1					4	3			118	125
Sick					1				1	1	3	4	1		47	57
Total	1		6	1	1	2	1	1	6	5	33	28	7	8	478	566

Copy. Original sent to the General, Oct. 21, 1778.

Signed   James Powell, Captain.

Field return of four companies of the third Circar battalion of Sepoys commanded by Captain James Johnstone, cantonments at Ellore, Oct. 16, 1778.

	Captain	Lieutenant	Enfign	Adjutant	Serjeant Major	Quarter-mafter Serjeant	Serjeants	Commandant	Subadar	Jemadar	Havaldars	Naikes	Drummers	Perchalls	Sepoys	Total
Field	1	1	2	1		1	2	1	5	5	19	18	6		259	313
Duty											4	3			48	55
Drill						1					2	5			92	99
Sick					1				1	1	3	6			30	41
Total	1	1	2	1	1	1	3	1	6	6	28	32	6		429	508

Copy. Original sent to the General, Oct. 21, 1778.

Signed   James Johnstone, Captain.

Translation

Tranflation of a letter from Pinnamanyanu Somanah and Baupinah Venkitachelem to Lingum Gowriah, Major Mathews's Dubafh, dated October 26, 1778.

Two guns that were conveyed from Samulcotah to Mafulipatam, and lately paffed from Ellore to Godevadah, for which we fupplied 350 bullocks, fifty buffaloes, and 300 coolies, and dragged the faid guns from Godevadah, to Mafulipatam Gate. We have not been paid any thing for the ufe of the cattle, nor Batta for the coolies; the latter was a charge out of our pockets. The bullocks and buffaloes were fo much injured by the heavy draft, that fince they were fo employed, they have been incapable of rendering us any fervice, moft of them having galled fhoulders: notwithftanding this misfortune we have not received one Cowry.

Tranflation of a letter from Daumarauze Mullaparauze Baamin Survinadoo, and Venkatapetty, inhabitants to Lingum Gowriah, Major Mathews's Dubafh.

We now addrefs ye, in hopes of obtaining payment for the expences we have been at for the company's people who travel backwards and forwards our road, and alfo the value of the bullocks we loft by conveying guns from here to Ellore. For fome time paft we have been fo much molefted by travellers, that we have had it under confideration to leave the place, and go far from oppreffion. But fince you have come to Ellore, we have been informed, that you have encouraged the neighbouring village people, near the road, to continue in their dwellings, and give them hopes, that whatever expence they are at, on the company's account, they will be repaid. Our people are much afraid, and cannot remain near the road; therefore I write to you, and you muft believe, that we write the truth. You will be fo good as to explain all this to your Mafter, ſter, and procure an order that we be paid what is our due. We were happy to hear that you are charitably difpofed; we, therefore, remain in our village, and addreſs you for relief. Whatever juſtice you do us will add to your reputation, and raiſe for you the eſteem of all our people.

Extract of a letter from Major Mathews's ſervant, Rajanah, to the Major, dated Ellore, Nov. 8, 1778.

Ragojee puntalu is not yet arrived from Maſulipatam. Lately the inhabitants, who had left their villages, went as far as Matuvelly to meet you; but you had paſſed the place before they arrived and went on to Bezwara. I believe that they will not venture to come here in your abſence; they are now near Matuvelly. Ragojee puntalu's ſervants tell every body that the letters which Major Mathews ſent to the chief and council of Maſulipatam, were all delivered to Ragojee puntalu; and that Anthony Sadleir had wrote to the Major that the Major had no buſineſs to interfere with Ragojee: copy of which letter was given to Ragojee, whoſe brother's ſon-in-law, by name Strepetty Saumey, ſaid all this, which, when the inhabitants heard, they went away beyond Wengalore. Ragojee puntalu's ſervants ſay, that after you received the abovementioned letter, you went away to Bezwara. Several people very earneſtly aſk me, why you do not come back again.

Extract of a letter from lieutenant Archibald Brown, dated Samulcotah, Nov. 11, 1778.

Rajanah-dourah, reſiding at Belgotu, in the Zemindary of Vizanagarum, with about one hundred and ſixty peons, did begin to aſſemble men, for the invaſion of the Tontapilly country, about the 20th of July; and having collected one hundred and fifty pikemen, from Wedady, with others from Vizanagarum, Anacapilla, and other

other villages, under Vizenagarum (in the diſtrict of Vizagapatam) in all amounting to about five hundred: with theſe, between the 1ſt and 5th of Auguſt (certainly not later than the 5th) he marched from Belgotum, twenty-four cofs, and took poſt at Raganagarum, or, in other words, the Pettah of Routlapunda fort, in which three hundred of Timrauze's people were ſtationed. There, having been joined by two hundred matchlock men, belonging to the village of Pettapoor, four hundred matchlock men, from the villages under Pettapoor; thirty matchlock men from Pedapoor, and other villages, under Timrauze; four hundred pikemen, from Pettapoor, and villages under it; one hundred pikemen, from Pedapoor, and villages under Timrauze; and four hundred bowmen, from the Tantapilly country. He remained about forty days, inveſting Routlapunda, and effectually ſtopped up its communication with the low country.

N. B. Belzotum belongs to Vizagapatam; Pettapoor and Pedapoor belongs to Maſulipatam, alſo the Tontapilly country.

Some Lombardy merchants, who were ſeized, and detained, in con‐
finement, by Mr. Hodges's ſervants, gave the following account of themſelves.

Nov. 28, 1778.

During the management of Jague-puntalu, he gave every ratifi‐cation to the Lombardys, the price of ſalt was nine anas for each pulla; a pulla is one hundred and twenty ſear; Garjane black ſalt, eight and a half per pulla; and, for every bullock load, he allowed waſtage, thirty ſear. We then uſed to go where we thought con‐venient, ſome to Maſulipatam, others to Nizamputam and Caracu‐cudu. But after that Chingleroy, who manages the ſalt buſineſs for Mr. Hodges, he received one dub more for every pulla, by way of cuſtom. Formerly we were allowed for every bullock, thirty ſear, by way of waſtage; he allows us only fifteen. We therefore think

it

it for our advantage to go to Pandarty salt-pans, where the price of salt, including the cuſtoms, is five Anas and two dubs, per putty. All the way to that place the road is very good, and we get to purchaſe ſalt from the Engliſh country. One duſtuck uſed to be given to a head-man of four or five hundred bullocks, at Nadaguda, for which we paid a rupee; but now for every hundred bullocks ſix Anas is demanded. Juſt before we were taken priſoners, a paper was brought to us ſignifying, that ſalt would be ſold, per putty, ſeven Anas, two and quarter dubs, and eighteen ſear allowed for waſtage. The goods that we had were to be received at the following rate.

Tamarind,	per putty,	Rupees	4	14 Anas.
Turmerick,	per maund,	ditto	1	1 ditto.
Mendaloo,	ditto,	ditto	2	4 ditto.
Paſſaloo,	per putty,	ditto	4	0

And while the agreement was writing, ſepoys came ſuddenly upon us and ſeized us; and we cannot tell what will be done with us and our goods. We beg that you will let us go to Pandarty, and we apply to you, becauſe you are a commander and we are priſoners. We have aſked Turmaling pilla for the Cowle that he wrote for us; and he replies, that he has not a Cowle, nor any other paper. Signed by the following merchants belonging to Hydrabad.

1 *Boorah,*	4 *Goindu,*
2 *Metoo,*	5 *Nauloo,*
3 *Kiſtnah,*	6 *Yacooroo.*

Captain Lane, to Major Mathews.

Sir,

I have been favoured with your's of the 28th, likewiſe, with two of the 30th ult. the contents of which ſhall be carefully attended to; a ſerjeant ſhall be diſpached to-morrow for Pentacotah.

After

After many evasions on the part of Peryrauze and repeated injunctions on mine, the Gulgunda man retired to his own country, by way of Shankarum on the 2d instant. A part of his followers (not amounting to more than 500, I have reason to conjecture, tho' these people call them 1000) were sent off on lieutenant Nelson's first joining them. A thousand still remained with him, till his final departure; the day before which Peryrauze himself and Rajanah-dourah patched up an accommodation between them, by which it is stipulated, that the latter is to receive a monthly allowance of 200 pagodas, and the Gulgunda man becomes a surety for his future good behaviour. The whole of this precipitate business was adjusted in one day's time, and Rajanah-dourah evacuated that part of the country on the following. By the last intelligence, he was retired to Ragapatnam, about twelve or more cofs from Totapilly. I am endeavouring to inform myself more particularly of the circumstances of this treaty, and of the present proceedings of Rajanah-dourah. As it has been already intimated to Peryrauze that he ought not to admit this man to terms, without the sanction of the company, who themselves would undertake the chastisement of him at a proper season. This treaty can be esteemed in no ways binding upon them in their future or present conduct towards him.

The circumstances that led to the Gulgunda man's appearing and taking an active part in this business are related to me as follows: and as I have collected this narrative from different quarters, I believe it to be authentic. When matters were last accommodated with Rajanah-dourah, a stipend of 200 pagodas per month, was engaged to him, and Godenrauze, then commandant of Vizramrauze's troops, became surety for his good behaviour. Godenrauze died, and from that time this allowance ceased also, though Rajanah-dourah failed not incessantly to reproach Timrauze's people with the injustice of detaining it from him. No regard, however, being paid to his claim, induced him to take up arms to assert his right, having no other means of subsisting his troops but by depredations. This is the apology he himself makes for his late conduct.

When Timrauze, then at the capital, became informed of this maroder's being in arms and committing devastations in the Totapilly country, he applied himself to Vizamrauze, telling him, that as he, in the person of his commandant, had in some measure become correspondent for Rajanah-dourah, it was incumbent on him to take measures for the again reducing him to subjection. In consequence of this, orders were sent to Vankatyrauze, the present commandant, and who is entrusted with the management of the country, in the absence of the two Rajahs, to interfere; and the Gulgunda troops were sent to reinforce Peryrauze in consequence. Perauze, expecting the return of the Rajah and apprehensive of the effects of his displeasure, determined to recover possession of the country by any plausible method he could fall upon: none appeared so eligible as the above, which, indeed, is only a renewal of the former agreements, which he is artful enough to perceive are by no means binding upon the company, whom he probably expects will still annul them, and at a favourable season undertake the final reduction of this man. In the mean time, his present purpose is answered. He is once more giving Cowl to the inhabitants, clearing away the Jungle, and thereby rendering Rajanah-dourah's usual lurking places more easy of access.

As circumstances may occur at Coringy, which it may be necessary you should have early intelligence of, I have instructed lieutenant Brown, in such cases, to correspond with you in your *public character*. The first coming through me would occasion much delay.

I am really without powder for the use of my recruits, and have only five port fires left, all of which are with Mr. Brown. I cannot avoid wishing, that you would consider these wants, and assist me with a moderate proportion of both. I have the pleasure to remain,

    Sir, your very obedient servant,

             Thomas Lane.

Samulcotah, Nov. 6, 1778.

P. S. I am waiting impatiently for the return of the grenadiers, in order to make out my general one.

Lieutenant Ruffel, to Major Mathews, commanding the troops in the Circars.

Sir,

The sepoys I sent yesterday morning to Newjure, returned this evening at eight o'clock; they went no further than Akkerapilly, where they met with Chelicauney Venkiah, and five hundred peons, on his way to Affuk Monickrow Jangana; they say, that he (Chelicauney Venhiah) is now at Muftabada, from whence he goes to Vedrupaulu, Terrygoppaula, Mauneycunda, and Meddour; at all these places he has relations, and expects to collect as many peons as will amount to five thousand, with which he intends to cross the river in nine days. At Akkerapilly the sepoys were informed that these peons are assembling with the approbation of the company for to assist Munickrow Jangana, which I imagine is a false report, as I understand Waffyreddy Ramanah is their tributary, and the other not. I send this letter by an extroadinary Tappy, and hope for your orders how to act by to-morrow evening; in the mean time, have sent sepoys to watch Chelicauney Venkiah, with directions to send me accounts of his motions. If the sepoys had not assured me, that there is no danger of his going across the river for some days, I would immediately detach a party to oppose his march; and if I receive any accounts, before your answer, that will, in my opinion, render that step necessary, shall do so; in hopes, that if I should

un-

unfortunately err, you will please, sir, to attribute it to my good wishes for the service.

I am, very respectfully, sir,

Your very humble servant,

James Russel.

Bezwara, Dec. 12, 1778.

Lieutenant Russel, to Major Mathews, commanding the troops in the Circars.

Sir,

Shortly after I had done myself the pleasure to address you this forenoon, a sepoy of the second battalion returned from Chentapilly, and says, that Wassyreddy's 6000 peons are now in the fort; also 100 horse: no horse is arrived there yet from Abram Beg. He says, that Monickrow is preparing to march to Chentapilly, and expects considerable reinforcements from Chelacauncy Venkiah. One of the sepoys that was after the latter is just now (3 P. M.) come in, and says, that Venkiah arrived this morning at Medoor with his 500 peons; in consequence of which I have directed lieutenant Forbes and his picquet to march immediately, as many of that company are detached and sick, I have directed him to take the command of serjeant Jolly's party and add to his own, which, with the number he takes from hence, will be more than sufficient to effect the business he goes on; for the sepoy assures me, that Chelacauncy Venkiah does not mean to cross the river these few days. I have desired Mr. Forbes to inform you of every thing material that occurs to him. Medoor is four cofs at this side of Cicacolum, and no boat there; but Sangrys, two cofs from hence, is one boat, for which I sent six sepoys, to see it brought hither.

I am, sir, your's, &c.

James Russel.

Bezwara, Dec. 14, 1778.

P. S.

P. S. Lieutenant Forbes's party will be eighty strong when he is joined by the serjeant's. It is now 4 P. M. and he is just marched.

Captain Lane, to Major Mathews, commanding the troops in the Masulipatam district.

Sir,

In Letters received from Lieutenant Brown, at Coringy, are the following paragraphs.

There are here two brass guns, country made, about 4lb. calibres, said to have been sold by Mr. Whitehill to the Holder of Samulcotah, when our troops were about to go against that fort, and again attached by orders of that gentleman before they were received. Be this as it may, I have reason to think they never have been carried to the company's account, and certainly are not private property. They never have been used, and as far as may be judged from outward appearance, seem excellent stout guns. One of them is spiked, the other half full of mud.

Dec. 21, 1778.

"In consequence of an order from the presidency to Mr. Hamilton, a few day since, to send the French subjects, now residing at Yanam, to Madras, the secretary and another inhabitant will embark to-morrow."

Both my armourers are at present ill with a fever, and incapable of doing any business. This prevents me for the present from complying with your order.

I am, sir,

Your very obedient servant,

Thomas Lane.

Samulcotab, *Dec.* 23, 1778.

Pro-

Proceedings of a Field Court-Martial, held by order of Lieutenant *James Ruffel*, at *Bezwara*, *Dec.* 31, 1778.

Lieutenant *Thompson*, President.

Ensign *M'calister* (Members) Ensign *Hazlewood*.

Prisoners. Faquier Arnot, Dene Mahomet, and Channs, sepoys confined by lieutenant James Ruffel, for disobedience of orders, and for imposition on several villagers.

Lieutenant James Ruffel informs the court, that, having orders for preparing to march, he directed his dubash to apply to the head men of the village for bullocks and coolies. The dubash informed him, that the assistance of sepoys would be necessary, and four were accordingly allowed for that purpose, on positive orders not to receive any batta from any of the village people, or inhabitants, as they should receive the company's batta for the time they were absent. On the 26th instant, serjeant Baine, of the first Circar battalion, told lieutenant Ruffel, that he apprehended that he was imposed upon by his dubash; and that he imagined it was the dubash's fault that the bullocks and coolies were not long since provided; for he was informed by one of the sepoys, who had been employed on that service, that some bullocks and coolies, which had been procured, were suffered to be sent back, in consideration of a pecuniary reward. Upon this lieutenant Ruffel sent for the sepoy, who confirmed what serjeant Baine had told him, also, that he, the sepoy, had received batta. Lieutenant Ruffel sent for his dubash, and asked, by what authority he released the bullocks, after they had been procured for the use of the service, and why he received any money from any of the village people on that account. He returned for answer, that it was no more than what was practised in this district

by

by every commanding officer's dubash; who, when they had collected as much as they could, gave it to their masters, who gave the dubash one rupee out of every pagoda; and such he meant to do by lieutenant Ruffel.

Serjeant Baine, of the first Circar battalion, informs the court, that on the 29th instant, he told Mr. Ruffel that he thought he was imposed upon by his dubash. Lieutenant Ruffel asked serjeant Baine if he had any proofs of what he had afferted. The serjeant replied, that one of the sepoys informed him, that the dubash had received money of the village people of Auloor. That the sepoy, who had been sent to procure bullocks and coolies, had several returned to the cantonments with some of the head men of different villages to the dubash, without informing lieutenant Ruffel; and the dubash always sent them back to the villages in the morning.

The Prisoner, Faquier Arnot, being put on his defence, says, that lieutenant Ruffel's dubash ordered him to procure bullocks and coolies. That on asking the villagers for bullocks and coolies, they told him, that they could not send either without having orders for that purpose from lieutenant Ruffel's dubash.

Question. From the court to the prisoner. Did any of the village people come with you to speak to the dubash?

Answer. There were ten head men of different villages came with me to speak to the dubash; but on meeting Major Mathews on the road, they received orders from him to proceed to Condapilly.

Question. Did you receive any money from any of the inhabitants of the villages that you went to?

Answer. Two of the peons with me received each one fanam; but I received none.

Question.

Question. Did the dubash order you to bring to the cantonments the head men of the different villages, if they did not give you bullocks and coolies.

Answer. He did.

Sentence. The court are of opinion the prisoner Faquier Arnot is guilty of the crime laid to his charge, on account of his denying receiving money from the villagers, and which has been proved against him; which, being a breach of the 2d Article of the 15th Section of the Articles of War, they do therefore sentence him to receive 200 lashes on his bare back, by the drummers of the detachment.

Prisoner. Dene Mahomet, private sepoy in the first Circar battalion, being put on his defence, says, that he received orders from lieutenant Ruffel's dubash to provide eight bullocks and eight coolies from different villages; that having got the bullocks, &c. he set out in order to bring them to the cantonments; but on receiving a letter from lieutenant Ruffel's dubash, he sent them back to the villages they belonged to. Having sent back the bullocks, &c. he came back to the cantonments, and went to the house of lieutenant Ruffel's dubash, who ordered him to leave his firelock there and come to him next morning, when he, the dubash, would send him to another place.

Question. From the court. Did you think it was the order of lieutenant Ruffel to send back the bullocks and coolies?

Answer. I did.

Question. Did you receive any batta from the village people, or inhabitants?

Answer. I received three fanams, and a peon, who was with me, received one fanam, two dubs, during the time I remained there, by order of lieutenant Ruffel's dubash.

Question. Do you think the dubash was impowered from Mr. Russel to allow this batta from the villages.

Answer. I did.

Question. Do you know whether any money was sent to the dubash of lieutenant Russel from any of the villages you went to?

Answer. I was at seven different villages, and one pagoda was sent from each, which I believe was sent to the dubash.

Question. Do you think it was in consideration of those seven pagodas that the bullocks, &c. were discharged.

Answer. I do.

Sentence. In consideration of the prisoner Dene Mahomet's obeying the orders of lieutenant Russel's dubash, the court do therefore acquit him.

Channo, a private sepoy in the first Circar battalion, being put on his defence, says, that he was ordered by the dubash of lieutenant Russel to procure from ten different villages twenty bullocks, twenty coolies, and ten cowry ropes. He set out from Abrampatam, and having shewn his dustuck to the head Vakeel, he was told, that what was mentioned therein should be got ready as soon as possible. Some time after, the head Vakeel told him, that in so small a village it was not possible for him to procure those several articles; but gave him six cowry ropes, and four coolies, which he, the sepoy, sent to the cantonments by a peon to the dubash of lieutenant Russel. After this the head Vakeel gave him three fanams, in consideration of an order from the dubash, and likewise gave to two peons, who went with him, two fanams, and one dub each, as batta. The head Vakeel desired the sepoy to go to some other place, as he the Vakeel would go to the dubash, and abide by his orders. After having procured seven buffaloes and two bullocks, he brought them to the cantonments.

Question.

Question. From the court. Did you receive any batta from the villages, or inhabitants of the places where you went to?

Answer. I received every day three fanams, and the two peons who were with me, two fanams and one dub each.

Question. Did you think it was the order of lieutenant Ruffel for you to receive the above batta from the villages?

Answer. I did.

Question. Do you know if any money was sent to the dubash of lieutenant Ruffel from any of the villages?

Answer. I do not know; but several of the head people of the villages came to speak to the dubash of lieutenant Ruffel, who afterwards ordered him to procure only two bullocks from each village.

Question. Did you receive those two bullocks from each village, in consequence of the orders of lieutenant Ruffel's dubash?

Answer. Having got two bullocks, I brought them to the Mosque on the Condapilly side of Bezwara hill, where I received a letter from lieutenant Ruffel's dubash, in which he ordered me to procure in every village two cowry of charcoal, which I understand was for the use of the dubash.

Question. Did not you know that it was the order of major Mathews, that no sepoys should receive any batta from any of the village people, when sent on service?

Answer. I did.

Sentence. In confideration of the prifoner Channo, abiding by the order of lieutenant Ruffel's Dubash, the court do therefore acquit him.

Lieutenant Ruffell's dubash being called,

Question.

Question. From the Court. What orders did you receive from lieutenant Ruſſell, when he deſired you to get the bullocks and coolies, he having orders to march?

Anſwer. My maſter, lieutenant Ruſſell, told me to get forty bullocks, fifty coolies and cowries.

Question. Did Lieutenant Ruſſell direct you to order the ſepoys to receive batta from the villages they went to?

Anſwer. He did not order me to tell the ſepoys to receive batta. On the contrary, gave me poſitive orders to tell them, on no account, to receive money from the inhabitants of the villages, as they would receive the company's batta on their return.

Question. Why did you order back the bullocks, after you had received your maſter's order to procure them?

Anſwer. The head men of Bezwara told me, that if I made out the duſtucks myſelf, the village people would run away; therefore, the head man deſired I would order back thoſe bullocks, &c. and he would provide lieutenant Ruſſel with whatever bullocks and coolies he might want.

Question. What anſwer did you give your maſter when he aſked, how or by whoſe order you received money of the village people?

Anſwer. It is what every commanding officer's dubaſh does; and the dubaſh, having collected as much as he can get, gives it to his maſter (the commanding officer) who allows the dubaſh one rupee in every pagoda; and ſuch I mean to do by my maſter, lieutenant Ruſſel.

Question. Did you ever hear of Major Mathews or his dubaſh receiving money or any other advantage from things of this kind?

Anſwer. I never did.

Question.

Question. Did you, ever since you lived with lieutenant Russell, receive any encouragement from him, that could give you reason to suppose he would be pleased by receiving advantages of this nature?

Answer. I never did.

Goindapah, a village man, being asked by the court, if he knew any thing of the several things mentioned here, corroborates what Dene Mahomet says; with this difference, that the money came for a head man of Bezwara, and not for the Dubash. And likewise says, that in consequence of the seven pagodas being sent, the bullocks were returned.

Question. To the prisoners, Faquier, Arnot, and Dene Mahomet. Did not you know, that it was the orders of major Mathews, that no sepoy should receive any batta from the villages, when out on service?

Answer. I did.

(Signed) *Andrew Thompson*, lieutenant of artillery, President.

Translation of a letter from Gobbeer Vencatrow, Hamaldar of Ongole, to Major Mathews.

I have received your letter, and understand it. Formerly, when the Lombardys came to Innacunda, and Audingy, the managers of the salt-pans of Pandarty, and those of Caracudu, used to give cowl to them; and then the merchants went to what salt-pans they liked. If they chose to go to Pandarty, the Peons of Caracudu would not molest them; and if they preferred Caracudu, the Peons of Pandarty would be no hindrance; and this was the method of conducting the business for near seventy years, which caused the managers of both places to agree; but, for the last three years, the Amuldars belonging to Mr. Hodges, Chingleroy, and Turnapilly,
forces

forces the merchants from Pandarty, and drives them to Caracudu; so that the merchants are not permitted to purchase salt at the place most convenient to them, but are compelled to take Mr. Hodges's salt at an advanced price. The long friendship that hath existed between the Nabob and the company, prevents us, his servants, from using the necessary power to do the inhabitants justice. The company's sepoys are always employed in carrying away the merchants from the Nabob's country, nor can the Lombardys find any redress but in bribing the guards, which sometimes they do to our injury another way, and drives the bullocks to demolish our growing corn; then, when the farmers complain, they are beaten, and their sheep are frequently stolen by open force. When you was in the district of Masulipatam, you were pleased to release the several Lombardy people that the sepoys had made prisoners, and told them to go to what salt-pans they pleased, according to the antient custom, and directed that in future the inhabitants should not be troubled, therefore I did not write to you. The English company will never do wrong, nor will the English gentlemen, but their servants behave very ill; and I beg of you to acquaint governor Rumbold of these transactions, that the merchants may, in future, go to what salt-pans they please, and that the droves of bullocks be allowed to travel in the usual roads, and that some compensation be made to the inhabitants for the loss they have suffered.

Dated at Ardingue, the 10th of February, 1779.

Sent to Major Mathews by the Nabob of the Carnatic, the 26th of March, 1779.

Salt has, for many hundred years been made in Pandarty and other ports belonging to the Carnatic, and in Nizamputtun, belonging to Masu-

Mafulipatam, to which places the Bungauras ufed of their own accords to go from the other fide of the river Kiftna, through the roads of Mortiffanagur and Polenaud, to purchafe falt; and thofe that went to Pandarty and other places, were not molefted or oppreffed by any of the people of Nizamputtun or Pandarty.

The Bungauras are fubjects who are merchants, and trade to whatever places they think may be moft for their intereft. The people of Nizamputtun do now, in contradiction to former cuftoms, fend fepoys to force the Bungauras, who are going to Pandarty and other places to purchafe falt, to go and buy it at that place. There is alfo a daroga with fepoys, in the diftrict of Pulnar, belonging to the Carnatic, who force the Bungauras from that fide the river Kiftna, to go to Nizamputtun, on which account they are become quite heartlefs, and will not go; and there will be a great lofs, on account of not felling the falt of Pandarty. It is very proper, that, according to antient cuftom, the Bungauras who trade to one place, fhould not, by force, be made to go to another. If the people of Nazamputtun, or Pandarty are defirous of a greater number of Bungauras, that they may difpofe of their falt the fooner, they fhould excite them by foft and perfuafive means, and they would then, of their own accord, go and purchafe the falt. Their proceeding by force and violence will be attended with the ruin of that place, and the falt will thereby be fpoiled, and will prevent the Bungauras from going there in future.

The village of Churlah is in the diftricts of Ongole, and the village of Punalah is in the diftricts of Nizamputtun, and they are both in the boundaries; and, to diftinguifh the grounds belonging to each village, ftones have, from antient times, been fixed: but, in the middle of the night, the people of Nizamputtun took away the ftones, and placed them in the middle of the village of Churlah, and laid claim to one half of the ground of the faid village; and,

not-

notwithstanding they endeavoured to prevent them from acting contrary to former customs, yet they would not adhere to them, but raised disturbances, and insisted on having half the ground and revenues of the said village.

The Circar will sustain great loss by their oppressions, and acting contrary to the former customs.

Translation of the account of the Ellore inhabitants, as given by Rajanah, a Bramin.

Rajanah, his account. Major Mathews sent for me, and ordered me to go to Vizceroy, (where the principal inhabitants had fled, to avoid the oppression of Ragogee-puntaloe) ; the Major directed me to take down in writing what they had to say. I went to them, and asked them the reason why they had left their villages ; they told me that Ragogee-puntaloo rented the Ellore Havally, and that he took both his own and the inhabitants share of the produce of the country, and buried it in the ground. He likewise increased the price of grain, and, by so doing, sundry expences of the villages increased. For these last three years, the country has been quite dry ; it was then under the management of Sobaram, who advanced money to the inhabiaants to go on with their cultivation, and that they likewise had balanced with Mr. Pringle ; at this time he managed the country, notwitstanding which, Ragojee obliged them to give a bond, in the paymaster's name, for all the balances of money, at the rate of three per cent. per month ; and that last year he encreased the price of grain still more, and for this year he took all the produce himself and buried it. He is now selling the grain which ought to be our property, for his own emolument ; he likewise reduced the price of our grain very low, and sold it himself at a high price, after which he wanted to settle accounts with us in the following manner, *viz.* Sadeevaur Andbadja, which signifies sundry accounts

counts of the villages. This is a part of our sufferings, and he sent peons every day to us to settle the above accounts. And because the company might not blame us for not going on with the cultivation, we borrowed money to buy seeds, and by that means carried on the cultivation of the country for this year, and we kept our own people to look after it. Our grievances are manifold, and oppressions obliged us to run away to a place where we could make our complaints in safety.

All they told me I wrote down, and it was signed by ten of the principal inhabitants, the whole of which I acquainted Major Mathews with. The Major then sent for the Muzzemdar, called Gazzevelly Venkatty Narm, and asked him if all this was true; that if it was, he would write to the board, and until the answer came, he advised them to return to their houses, and to go on with the cultivation of the country, and desired the Muzzemdar to tell the inhabitants so; after which I went with the Muzzemdar to the inhabitants: first, they said that they would go, then again, that Ragojee puntalu was gone to Masulipatam to ruin them; and on his return they do not know how he will use them. Then they said to me, your master is not a going to stay at Ellore, therefore, if we stay in our villages, we are sure of being oppressed by Ragojee puntalu. If, after the Major has received orders concerning us, and he and Ragojee will promise to do us justice, then we will come; but not unless the Major be present; for we are afraid to trust ourselves with Ragojee: so we will go to Worgore, and remain there until orders come from the board.

At the time they sent their petition they desired me to tell Major Mathews, that he and the paymaster were of one cast, and that Ragojee puntalu belonged to the paymaster; therefore, if the Major chose to believe what Ragojee says, sooner than what we say, he had

better

better return our petition. They are gentlemen, and we are poor people; they are able to make presents. We have lost all our profits and are turned poor, therefore, if he is unwilling to take our business in hand, we require you to return our petition.

All the above I told the Major's dubash, that he might acquaint him of it. In consequence of the petition the Major sent me and the Muzzemdar to persuade the inhabitants to return to their villages; but was answered that Ragojee puntalu would bring some fresh accusations against them, from the chief and council of Masulipatam; so they were afraid to return to their villages, but said, that they would stay in some of the villages near the place. And I Rajanah do declare, that to the best of my knowledge, Major Mathews did not desire them to make any complaint; nor does the Major know them, or they him.

Translation of the account of the Ellore inhabitants, as given by Selar Mahomed, a Peon.

Selar Mahomed, his account. Peddapaudoo and Rauzepettah, two villages in the Ellore country, the inhabitants of which having quarrelled, the inhabitants of Rauzepettah came and complained to Major Mathews; on which the Major sent the above-named peon to go and enquire into the particulars of their quarrel, and on his arrival there, he found that all the principal inhabitants had abandoned their village. On my road back I stopped at a place called Matlore, where I asked, for what reason the principal inhabitants abandoned their village. I was told that Ragojee puntalu (the renter) and they could not agree; and that yesterday Ragojee sent a party of peons after the inhabitants, which obliged them to fly into Nariah's country, but they could not tell to what part. All this I acquainted Major Mathews with; he then desired I would carry a letter to the fugitives,

fugitives, and if poffible perfuade them to come to him; but if they did not chufe to come, then to bring back an anfwer to the letter fent them.

I went and delivered the letter to the principal inhabitants, who were at a place called Vizceroy; this was about three in the afterternoon. When they had read the letter, they gave me an anfwer to it, and told me, that as Major Mathews was a great man, he ought to fend fome principal perfon to them to whom they might explain their grievances, and to do them juftice, and then they would come, if not, they would leave the country and never return. On this I returned and delivered their letter to the Major, and told him what they had defired me. And I Selar Mahomed do declare, that to the beft of my knowledge, that before this time they knew nothing of Major Mathews, nor he of them, and that he did not perfuade them to complain.

THE END.

www.ingramcontent.com/pod-product-compliance
Lightning Source LLC
Chambersburg PA
CBHW020759230426
43666CB00007B/769